Careers Education to Demystify Employability

Careers Education to Demystify Employability

A Guide for Professionals in Schools and Colleges

Kate Daubney

Open University Press

Open University Press
McGraw Hill
8th Floor, 338 Euston Road
London
England
NW1 3BH

email: enquiries@openup.co.uk
world wide web: www.openup.co.uk

First edition published 2021

A catalogue record of this book is available from the British Library

ISBN-13: 9780335250943
ISBN-10: 0335250943
eISBN: 9780335250950

Library of Congress Cataloging-in-Publication Data
CIP data applied for

Typeset by Transforma Pvt. Ltd., Chennai, India

Praise page

An essential read for all Careers Leaders, Careers professionals and teachers involved in the delivery of careers work in schools and colleges. It provides a clear and comprehensive overview of the issues surrounding Careers and Employability while offering a fresh perspective on how to tackle the challenges faced by Careers professionals working with young people. Highly recommended!

Jodie Boyd, Senior Lecturer and Course Leader for the MA Career Development and Employability and PGCert Career Leadership, University of Huddersfield, UK

As someone delivering postgraduate, professional education to new and current careers and employability professionals in Higher Education, Schools and FE; I warmly welcome Kate's important contribution to cross-sector knowledge exchange. It provides access to valuable learning from research and practice in the HE sector in ways which are practically applicable for colleagues in Schools and FE.

Dr. Bob Gilworth, Senior Lecturer in Careers Guidance, School of Education and Professional Development, University of Huddersfield, UK

Back Cover

It provides a clear and comprehensive overview of the issues surrounding Careers and Employability while offering a fresh perspective on how to tackle the challenges faced by Careers professionals working with young people. Highly recommended!

Jodie Boyd, Senior Lecturer and Course Leader for the MA Career Development and Employability and PGCert Career Leadership, University of Huddersfield, UK

I warmly welcome Kate's important contribution to cross-sector knowledge exchange. It provides access to valuable learning from research and practice in the HE sector in ways which are practically applicable for colleagues in Schools and FE.

Dr. Bob Gilworth, Senior Lecturer in Careers Guidance, School of Education and Professional Development, University of Huddersfield, UK

This book is dedicated to anyone who wants to discover what they are capable of, including Will, Krem, Charlie, and Elaina who all took a path less travelled.

This book is also, as always, for L.

Contents

About the author

Kate Daubney has been an educator for almost thirty years, working as an academic, a researcher, a teacher, and a careers professional. She has worked in seven different United Kingdom universities including post-92 and Russell Group institutions, and has been specialising in Careers education for almost twenty years, working with pre-18 learners, university students, mid-career professionals, postgraduate researchers, and the globally mobile. She is a qualified teacher in higher education, she has trained school teachers, has also worked in schools and with schools and school teachers on careers education for many years. She has been an invited keynote speaker at a number of UK and international conferences, including for the Universities and Colleges Admissions Service (UCAS), and in the USA, Denmark, and Australia.

Kate was Director of Careers & Employability at the University of Chester before becoming Head of Careers & Employability at King's College London on behalf of the University of London in 2017. In late 2020 she was appointed as Director of The Careers Group, the federation of careers services of the University of London, and as Director of the University of London's new Centre of Excellence in Careers and Employability. She is a Principal Fellow of the Higher Education Academy, and has a doctorate in film music. Her research in Careers education and Employability development has been published in peer-reviewed journals, and she is recognised internationally for her innovations in extracting Employability from the curriculum and Careers learning gain, which are explored in this book.

List of Figures

Preface

This book was planned during the autumn of 2019, and was written during the early weeks of the first Coronavirus lockdown in the UK, in the spring of 2020. While writing the book, there was a flood of media attention around how the crisis might impact the short- and longer-term employment prospects of learners, students, and graduates, and as 2020 continued, the realities of the economic impacts of the pandemic have become more widespread and more damaging. Current speculation suggests that an entire generation of young people could have their prospects damaged. And some of the sectors most dominant in the UK economy such as creative professions, hospitality, tourism, and retail have been decimated, so the outlook feels bleak.

Labour markets can be tricky things to predict at the best of times. There is a wealth of data out there, much of it reported on in quite dramatic terms by the media. At the start of 2021, the UK government produced a new White Paper on Skills that is intended to contribute to the economic recovery through further education and greater employer collaboration. But the danger is that in a fast-moving and unpredictable economic and technologically driven landscape, a focus on specialist Skills that makes sense at one point in time can date very quickly. There is already a sense that the Fourth Industrial Revolution has been significantly accelerated by the social and economic change created by the pandemic. So what *does* the future hold?

Careers educators know, however, that whatever the landscape, one truth remains: if you have an idea of where you are heading with your Career, and you know yourself and what you offer well, you are much more likely to reach your destination, even if the route is a bit more complicated than you had hoped. That truth transcends all else that might happen, and at a time of change we need consistency and coherence to support our learners and students. We need core approaches to how we talk about and develop learners' and students' Careers decision-making and how we enable them to recognise and develop their Employability.

This book will help you do that better. It is not a direct response to the pandemic, but the ideas it explores are more relevant than ever in the world the pandemic has shaped of digital compression and economic and employment fragility. It has never been more challenging to support young people to find their way, so this book is designed to help Careers Leaders, Careers professionals, and teachers in schools and colleges get more impact out of what they are already doing. Putting in place the infrastructure of thinking, understanding, and self-awareness that enables learners to know where they are on their Career journeys, and to identify and articulate what they bring to the job market through their academic learning, are both fundamental to navigating a difficult and unpredictable landscape. I hope this book helps you do that for your learners.

Kate Daubney
February 2021

Acknowledgements

The Careers profession is an extraordinarily generous environment to work in. I am constantly overwhelmed by colleagues' generosity in discussing, sharing, exploring, critical-friending, and imagining. In particular, I have benefited from the community of the professional body of careers in higher education, the Association of Graduate Careers Services (AGCAS). After every meeting, conference, or phone call with a colleague I leave thinking differently, and that level of support makes everyone's work more impactful for students and learners.

I want to say particular thanks to my colleagues at King's Careers & Employability, both present and past, who have done so much to enable thousands of students to make progress in their Career journeys and Employability development. While I was deployed to King's as Head of King's Careers & Employability by the University of London, they inspired me by being a highly collaborative team, embracing every idea and initiative I came up with, and exploring what was possible so that our students would benefit. I also want to acknowledge the work of Tisha Pryor, Sue Moseley, and Morag Walling, who developed In With From, from which I evolved the model In Around Beyond (shared in this book) for a school and college purpose.

Dr Bob Gilworth, former President of the Association of Graduate Careers Advisory Services and former Director of The Careers Group, not to mention the person who twice appointed me to be a Head of Careers, has been a most generous critical friend. He has long been an advocate of maps and luggage on Careers journeys, and was the first person who I heard say that it was easier not to be lost if you knew where you were starting from. He and Dr Nalayini Thambar developed the Careers Registration process from which I derived the Three Stage Journey model discussed in this book, and they transformed the HE Careers landscape permanently in doing so. You can find out more about that in Appendix 4.

My thanks also to the many, many colleagues at the many universities in the UK, Europe, Canada and the USA, the Middle East, Australia and New Zealand who have invited me to share my work on Careers learning gain and Extracted Employability over the past few years, and thus have given me hours of peer review, stimulating discussion, challenge, exploration, testing, and reflection. If these concepts were cars, consider them thoroughly road- and crash-tested.

But a few colleagues and former students and friends have also taken more than their fair share of the discussion burden in making me think better and harder and differently. Huge, huge thanks to all of you. I am sure I have missed too many names off this list, but in roughly alphabetical order you are:

Danny Wilkey-King

Dympna Nightingale and Karen Scimia

Eluned Jones

Gemma Green

Gill Frigerio and Angela Vesey

Jakob Krummes at the University of Southern Denmark, Rikke Jónson at Aalborg University, and the careers professionals of the University of Copenhagen

James Darley

Jane Campbell and Sarah Wenham

Jodie Boyd

Lynne Barker and Tom Atterson

Mark Colvenbach and Tim Harding

Michael Healy

My colleagues at The Careers Group and Professor Mary Stiasny OBE

My students at the University of Derby, including all the trainee teachers I had the privilege to teach at the start of their careers

My terrific team in Careers & Employability at the University of Chester

Philip Blair and the careers professionals of the East Kent network

Saj Jetha

Will Allott, Charlie Duckworth, Krem Ferris, James Plaut, Theodora Briggs

I would like to thank Eleanor Christie, Beth Summers, and Zoe Osman at the Open University Press for a very supportive and practical editorial process, which took place while I was starting a new job and doing a postgraduate qualification. Your enthusiasm for this project has been exceptional and I'm incredibly grateful. Thanks also to Dave Cummings for copyediting the script.

I also want to give a specific and enormous thank you to the incredibly gifted Kalina Zlatkova, an exceptional illustrator, who took my hopeless diagrams and turned them into graphics that I hope you find accessible and usable. Her talents are far beyond what you see in this book, and this book is far better for her talents. You can find more of her illustrations and work at http://kzlatkova.co.uk – thank you, Kalina!

List of abbreviations

AGCAS Association of Graduate Careers Advisory Services
AI   Artificial intelligence
BTEC   Business and Technology Education Council
CDI   Career Development Institute
FE   Further education
GCSE   General Certificate of Secondary Education
HE   Higher education
ISE   Institute of Student Employers
OECD   Organisation for Economic Co-operation and Development
PSHE   Personal, Social, Health, and Economic education
STEM   Science, Technology, Engineering, and Mathematics
UCAS   Universities and Colleges Admissions Service
VLE   Virtual Learning Environment

A note to education policy-makers

Dear Colleague,

I know you have had a really challenging time since the start of the pandemic, and I would not be writing to you directly at the very start of this book if I didn't have something important to share, that I think can really make a difference to the future of the young people so dramatically impacted by this crisis.

This book was not written for you: it was written for Careers Leaders, Careers professionals, and teachers, and I do not expect you to have the time to read the whole thing yourself. But this letter is to direct you to the most relevant parts of this book to help you do something sustainable, consistent, and transformational through your role as policy-makers in pre-18 education to enable learners to make the connection between their academic study and work, and thus to make that transition more easily. It will not require an enormous investment or the creation of a new portfolio of qualifications. It will not require you to gaze into a crystal ball and guess what specialist Skills will be needed next. It proposes that we recognise in an infrastructural but easy-to-deliver way the role that transferable Skills and not specialist Skills play in enabling life-long agility and flexibility across different roles, professions, and careers.

The Skills Unit of the Organisation for Economic Co-operation and Development has published research on the importance of embedding transferable Skills development in pre-18 education.[1] At a conference in early 2021, I asked Glenda Quintini, Senior Economist in the Skills Unit, whether any progress had been made on this. She said, 'No.'

That is simply not acceptable. Even without the devastating economic impacts of the pandemic, we have a moral and ethical imperative to make the transition from education to work clearer and easier for learners. It is a key element in supporting the most marginalised and challenged learners in our society, and it works in every educational system.

So if you are an education policy-maker anywhere in the world, do not wait a moment longer to do this. We are experiencing a world-defining economic crisis that is already damaging an entire generation of young people's prospects, but you have an opportunity to do something that will improve their situation by making the connection between the pre-18 curriculum and work clear.

This is what you have to do:

1 If you have a whole day, read all of this book.
2 If you have two hours, read the Challenges (pp. 8–15), Environment (pp. 16–21), and Employability Introduction (pp. 101–4) and Skills (pp. 126–45) sections.

3 If you have 60 minutes, read the Skills section (pp. 126–45).

4 If you have 30 minutes, read instead my peer-reviewed journal article which summarises the whole Employability section and research, and indicates what needs to be done.[2]

And if you are only reading this note, then please recognise this: if we rewrite curriculum documentation to make explicit the transferable Skills innate to each subject of study, then in every syllabus derived from that we transform fundamentally the ability of learners to see how pre-18 education connects to work. That is all you have to do. I have done the research, I have the information you need. Just get in touch with me and I'll help you get it done.

So if you care even one bit about transforming the lives of young people and giving them a fighting chance to withstand whatever economic, social, and technological changes are coming, you will make this simple but fundamental addition to curriculums and enable teachers to bring out additional value from what they teach. You can join up existing fundamental qualification structures with work and Careers without having to create new qualifications or programmes. And without asking teachers to do anything differently other than simply flag up the Skills learners use when they use them in real time in the classroom. That's it.

Just do it. No excuses, please. It is not difficult. But it will change everything. Thank you.

Kind regards

Kate

Notes

1 Organisation for Economic Co-operation and Development (2019) *Getting Skills Right: Future-Ready Adult Learning Systems*, Paris: OECD Publishing. Available at: https://doi.org/10.1787/9789264311756-en.

2 Article available at: https://www.emerald.com/insight/content/doi/10.1108/JWAM-08-2020-0041/full/html.

Introduction: Welcome!

Welcome to *Careers Education to Demystify Employability!*

This book is principally for Careers Leaders, Careers professionals, and teachers in UK schools and colleges, many of whom have to follow UK government statutory guidance on Careers delivery. But I think this book will also be useful to parents and learners themselves, from anywhere in the world and at any stage in a life-long educational journey, because the fundamental ideas about how we talk about Career journeys, and how we enable young people to make the transition into work, are fairly similar wherever and whoever you are.

Because this book is principally for Careers educators and subject educators, it has quite a bit of content on how to shape learning in Careers and Employability. And along the way there is some signposting about how the different ideas fit into the different Benchmarks for Good Career Guidance that currently form the basis of the statutory guidance. But if you are also reading this as a parent or even as a learner at any age early teens upwards, hopefully some of the ideas make sense in their own right. Furthermore, as my note in the front matter indicates, if you are an education policy-maker, you will also find some strong hints as to how to look at educational experiences for adolescent learners differently! Some of the factors I explore in this book that affect learners negatively would be easily resolved by some small but fundamental changes to the ways in which curriculum is presented to learners and choice is represented and measured.

I wrote this book because as a Careers professional who has worked in higher education (HE) in a range of different roles, and most recently as a head of a Careers service in two very different universities, I have had the privilege to explore, develop, shape, and test ideas that really make a difference to learners. In reality, as we will see later, undergraduate students in their late teens and early twenties face exactly the same concerns, dilemmas, and confusion as 11–18-year-old learners. The age distinction is, in my experience, really an arbitrary one created by a change of phase in education or work. So I think there is a huge amount that can be shared from well-resourced, effectively tested, and peer-evaluated work in HE Careers services that can really make a difference to pre-18 learners in schools and colleges. This book captures some of that thinking, but you can also find out more about HE Careers education through the Association of Graduate Careers Advisory Services (AGCAS), the professional body for HE Careers.

There is a lot of material and resources out there about how people make Career decisions, about what the employment market looks like, and lots of tools online to help align learner interests with future Career possibilities. So I think it is helpful to start off by being clear about what this book is, and what it isn't.

This book offers:

- Clarity about what we mean when we say 'Careers' and 'Employability' – words which not every learner or teacher (or parent or employer or education policy-maker) will be familiar with or understand confidently
- A new way of looking at the key stages at which young people have to make Careers decisions and the issues that arise in making the transition to work or further study
- Some ideas about how to address those issues that will provide your learners with a strong backbone to their future Careers decision-making
- A learner-facing way of talking about Employability that joins up education and work
- A capture of some of the most impactful ideas being used in HE Careers education and Employability development that are relevant and usable in schools and colleges
- Some suggestions of how schools and colleges can maximise the benefit of every teacher's interaction with every learner, to support good Careers decision-making and the preparation for the next stage, whatever that is
- Some ideas about how learners can understand better the transition to university and to work, and how you can help them prepare for those transitions.

This book does not provide:

- A list of resources and tools you can find online to help you deliver the statutory guidance
- A Benchmark-by-Benchmark solution for a good Careers programme (though you will find content here that supports many of the Benchmarks)
- A scholarly study of best practice (though there are some references at the end that will be worth reading).

This book is divided into sections, so you can dip in and out, but I would recommend reading it through in order first because the solutions make more sense if you can get to grips with the problems.

In **Part 1: Context**, I start by asking why it matters to find better ways to talk to learners about Careers and Employability, and I outline some of the **Challenges** young people face in making decisions about their future. I also map out the **Environment** learners are navigating. You can share all of this thinking with learners, parents, and teachers, and hopefully they will help you and your learners identify and put a name to some of the issues your learners are experiencing in their Careers decision-making and Employability development. I finish setting the context by digging down into what we mean when we talk about **Careers** and **Employability**. Because being clear about that is fundamental to helping learners make progress and own their own choices and development.

In **Part 2: Careers**, I introduce a way of thinking about Careers journeys that will dovetail very neatly into any existing programme of Careers education you have in your school or college, and will certainly tie into any understanding you might have about Career theories. But you do not need any understanding of Careers education or Careers guidance to find the ideas proposed here useful and accessible. I introduce the **Three Stage Journey** and then take you through ten Activities that will provide a range of innovative ways to maximise the benefit of what you are already doing in your school or college Careers programme in order to get more impact for your learners. These include enabling learners to self-identify where they are on their Careers journey, recognise the value of different interactions, and show how to create meaningful work experiences, including virtually.

As I outline in **Part 3, Employability** development is only superficially understood in pre-18 education, even in more technical qualifications and study programmes, let alone in the statutory guidance, and much of the excellent content that is being delivered to engage learners with employers and enterprise is focused more on work than making a connection to learners' existing educational experiences. The content in Part 3 joins education and work together, and provides a way of talking about Employability that is meaningful to all learners at all ages on all types of qualifications. By exploring how studying curriculum develops Knowledge, Attributes, Skills, and Experience in learners, I share a range of ideas for Activities and ways to talk about Employability to your learners, and introduce the findings of some research I have done which will help you talk about this to your learners. I also introduce a model for helping learners understand the relationship between the subject Knowledge and Careers choices through Employability. I summarise Parts 2 and 3 by reflecting in **Part 4: Overcoming the Challenges** how the approaches explored, particularly with relation to Employability, address the issues identified in the Context section.

Part 5 explores **Transitions** for learners into both higher education and work. I also reflect on the role of digital Skills in the workplace and how to help learners recognise the similarities and differences to their existing use of digital Skills. I conclude the book by reflecting on coping with **Uncertainty and Ambiguity**, a key Attribute that learners will need to develop if they are to navigate this uncertain landscape.

I hope you find this book useful. As Careers professionals and teachers, we are often the temporary custodians of the hopes, aspirations, and dreams of our learners when they share them with us. In their early stages, those dreams are often as fragile as freshly blown soap bubbles. So it is a privilege to be able to share the work I have developed to try to make those bubbles a little less fragile, and to help you feel more confident when they alight in your hands.

How to use this book

In **Part 2: Careers** and **Part 3: Employability**, I introduce a range of **Activities** that you can work through, all of which are about getting more value and impact for learners from what you are already doing in your school or college Careers programme, and many of which should offer new ideas. You do not have to do all of them. You may want to do some of them but not be resourced in staff, time, or money to do others. But hopefully you can see how everything fits together and how benefit becomes cumulative across the Activities. Anything you do that you aren't already doing will make a difference to your learners. In each section, I will make clear which are the most useful activities you could do, if you are short on capacity.

Each Activity includes:

- Key principles for you: these summarise why and how this Activity is useful
- Messages for learners: these are simple, consistent points that join the Activities together and reinforce the thinking we would like learners to develop
- Actions: the steps you can take to do this Activity
- Context value: for those whose schools and colleges need to follow the statutory guidance, each Activity concludes with indicators about which Benchmarks are met by the elements of the Activity.

Part 1

Context

Why does it matter to find better ways to talk to learners about Careers and Employability?

Even without a global pandemic in the picture, I think there are a number of factors that have come together in recent years that mean it is more important than ever to find better ways to talk to learners about Careers and Employability. In no particular order, I have repeatedly encountered the following factors, and while not all of them may apply to you and your learners, my many conversations with teachers and Careers educators indicate that you are likely to recognise at least one of these:

- There is increasing research about how young people's neuroscientific make-up is a factor in their decision-making, but not much application yet for how this impacts their Careers decision-making
- Strongly voiced frustrations by teachers that they are struggling to engage learners with Careers within a paralysing educational framework that seems to hinder, not help
- Statutory guidance and Benchmarks which, while well-meaning, focus on processes and expectations and do not always support effective ways to engage learners
- A bit of a gulf between the relatively well-resourced, evidence-led practice of Careers education and Employability learning in UK higher education, and the ability of the school and college sector to benefit from it.

And it matters that we find a way to address the negatives and harness the positives for two main reasons:

- Young people are more likely to be successful at the next stage if they go into it with a clear understanding of their Careers and Employability journeys, and how everything they gain at this stage opens up opportunities at the next
- Teachers and Careers educators in school need more impact from their efforts to help make this possible.

What are the Challenges young people face in making decisions about their future?

I think there are five main challenges that young people face, that make the decision-making process through school, college, and beyond more difficult than we would like. Some of these can be addressed and resolved, and some mitigated. In the next few pages, I'm going to outline what I think those five challenges are, but here they are for starters:

Challenge 1: The Hourglass Phenomenon

Challenge 2: Qualifications as Knowledge Assets

Challenge 3: Paralysis

Challenge 4: Narrowing definitions of success

Challenge 5: The Neuroscience of the adolescent brain

Throughout the book I will refer to which of these Challenges I think the ideas here can help with, but you are likely to see some other value yourself for your school or college context, and through the learners you are working with too.

Challenge 1: The Hourglass Phenomenon

The Hourglass Phenomenon captures one of the earliest journeys that learners go on. A learner studying in the UK, from the age of about 11, becomes aware that they are steadily reducing the number of subjects they are focusing on as they get older. But the reality is that the number of Career options on offer to that learner remains at least constant or might expand. In my experience of working with thousands of learners of all ages, making the transition from reduction to expansion at the narrowest part of the hourglass is a really crippling place to pass through if you are a learner.

Figure 1. The Hourglass

Illustration by Kalina Zlatkova. © Kalina Zlatkova 2021.

In my experience, the Phenomenon has two phases:

Phase 1: Inbound : A narrowing academic framework

Up to and beyond the age of 18 into higher education, the academic framework in the UK creates the following situations for learners, by increasingly narrowing the choices learners must make in the context of this structure.

Figure 2. A linear journey

Illustration by Kalina Zlatkova. © Kate Daubney 2021.

In this dynamic:

- Learners often perceive that 'a wrong choice' will rule out future options, creating a 'one-way' street in Careers terms, possibly leading to a dead end
- Learners experience decision-making points about qualifications and learning as fixed and rigid, so they make decisions under the pressure of a ticking clock
- Learners lack the experience on which to draw to make decisions well (see **Challenge 5** also)
- Career choice is presented as linear: 'if you want to do Career X, you must do subject combination Y'.

Phase 2: Outbound : An explosion of choice

But on the other side of each of those stages, when a stage of education is completed at the secondary, tertiary, or higher level of education by taking particular qualifications, Career choice expands enormously, not just with respect to what type of activity comes next (more study, work, or a combination of the two) but also with what that activity might be.

Figure 3. Multiple possible outcomes

Illustration by Kalina Zlatkova. © Kate Daubney 2021.

Key factors include:

- In the majority of cases, employers do not have a preference for qualifications as a prerequisite for entry to a role or Career path, so the Knowledge/qualification specialism will not be a significant factor in recruitment

- Many study choices post-16 and at university do not have specific qualification prerequisites, opening up new curriculum choices
- The Knowledge content of qualifications is often not directly relevant to Career choices available to learners
- Learners have little idea what else they bring to the next phase of their journey, particularly work, other than qualification-based Knowledge
- Paradoxically, good Career guidance encourages students to understand and own their own definition of Career success, which is not generally rooted in qualifications
- All Career outcomes are, theoretically, available to all learners in these early phases of Careers – it is just that the route to get there may be longer, more circuitous, or require some adjustment or compromise along the way.

These two phases together result in a period of incredible compression when decisions are made, which creates other issues at the next stage.

Challenge 2: Qualifications as Knowledge Assets

Qualifications at school, college, and university level are largely presented as Knowledge Assets. In other words, their value is described in terms of what is learned.

- We ask: 'What subjects do you study?'
- We ask learners to make decisions in relation to Knowledge prerequisites: 'You will need to have studied Chemistry if you want to be a vet'.

But that creates a perception for learners that Knowledge is a linear gain: 'If I know X, then I can do Y'. This is sometimes true in academic terms, because there are affinities between subjects that may aid learners in transitioning into new subjects: Maths into Physics, History into Politics, and so on.

But in taking this approach, we create two consequences which become unhelpful for learners when they are trying to think beyond linear Knowledge-based connections.

1 We create an assumption in the learner that any future choice must be related to something they are already familiar with – and by extension if they are not familiar, it will be a far harder learning journey.
2 We obscure the idea that there might be any other connections between subject learning that have value in other contexts such as the workplace, or which might connect subjects together in what seem to be less linear ways.

A great example of this is something I will come back to later in more detail when we talk about Employability, but I will pose the question now:

> *Why did one global business recruit more graduates of History to become tax auditors than from any other subject?*

And while you are thinking about that, ask yourself when was the last time that you suggested to a History student in your school, college, or wider acquaintance that they were well suited to a Career in tax audit. It is a great example of why challenging the perception of qualifications as Knowledge Assets is so important to supporting learners to make good Career decisions.

Challenge 3: Paralysis

Something I hear very often from Careers Leaders, Careers professionals, and teachers in schools and colleges, but also from Careers professionals across higher education, is that learners aged anywhere between the early teens to early twenties often feel absolutely paralysed during what feel like the most crucial Careers decision-making phases of their lives. There are two main reasons for this:

1. Paralysis by possibilities

I touch on this above with the Hourglass Phenomenon, but I am sure many of us will have heard something like this from a learner:

> *There are so many things I could do, so many subjects I could choose, I don't know where to begin, and what if I get it wrong and what if I hate what I choose or I'm not very good at it, and what if I can't decide what to do after and what if...*

In higher education, there are costs attached to this conversation too, the costs of a university education whether that includes fees or not. So this sort of paralysis feels incredibly burdensome to the learner whether they are in higher education or considering entering it. But as the time dynamic of the world becomes more immediate, there is also the perceived cost of lost time, and the fear of one individual's decisions taking them out of sync with another's.

2. Paralysis by process

This is implied by our learner's worries above: *what if I get it wrong?* The key moments at which the Hourglass Phenomenon bites – post-secondary, post-tertiary, post-HE – are rigidly prescribed and controlled. A combination of tight timetables and a long annual cycle means that learners are not only navigated to make what are presented as critical future decisions with long-term impacts at very limited times, but the consequences are also presented as linear.

If they get it wrong in that narrow window, they will have missed the boat to explore other choices or take a different route. And they must wait another year or take a less satisfactory choice to compensate for that. This means that learners are less inclined to take time to explore their options or take what might seem like a more 'risky' choice outside the linear connections described in **Challenge 2.**

Challenge 4: Narrowing definitions of success

Definitions of success for learners have effectively become narrower, with schools and colleges being measured on the destinations of their learners. So it is inevitable that learners will be impacted when their place of learning is being evaluated against specific outcomes. This is already a factor in higher education and how universities are evaluated with the destinations of leavers being measured against a model of success defined by a 'graduate' outcome (for example, a barrister) as opposed to a non-graduate outcome (for example, a barista).

Coupled with that, we know from higher education that learners are often strongly influenced by the choices of their peers (see also **Challenge 5: The Neuroscience of the adolescent brain**). For example, if a learner is unsure about what sort of graduate scheme to choose, they will often look to their more decisive peers and choose accordingly. In practice, learners who make a self-aware, self-informed choice are more likely to be successful in their longer-term Careers choices, but when the 'atmospheric pressure' drives immediate choices (see *Paralysis by process* above) made from established 'success' outcomes (e.g. university at post-18, graduate recruitment schemes at post-HE), it is not surprising that uncertain learners will be influenced by the decisions of their peers. If those choices are already narrow in scope, learners may find themselves inadvertently making a choice that is less successful for them than it might be for their peers. Of course, the reverse might be true, but the way in which learning institutions present 'good' choices to learners certainly affects their Careers decision-making.

So broadening definitions of success and removing some of the narrative around linearity being inevitable are really valuable here. Learners who shape and own their definitions of Careers success are much more likely to keep to them, and maximise the value of opportunities that arise through them.

In 2018, there was a change to how the employment outcomes of graduates was measured, with one very specific feature that will start to address this. When graduates are now surveyed, 15 months after the end of their degree, they are asked to determine to what extent they agree with the following statements:

* My current work/study fits with my future plans
* My current work/study is meaningful (to you, to others, to society at large).

It remains to be seen how long it will take for changes to measurement to shape changes to narratives, and how quickly universities, rankings, and policy-makers decide that the graduate's own definition of success is the one most worth measuring. But when the new survey dataset came out for the first time, those were the first answers I most wanted to see. Because really they should be the only ones that matter.

Challenge 5: The Neuroscience of the adolescent brain

If you haven't read Sarah-Jayne Blakemore's excellent and fascinating book *Inventing Ourselves: The Secret Life of the Teenage Brain*, I highly recommend it. It is a readable and insightful guide to how the neuroscientific functions of adolescents influence and shape their behaviour. For educators, particularly those trying to help learners to engage with decision-making, Blakemore's chapters on the impact of relationships and attitudes towards risk are really valuable indicators of some of the factors that influence how learners in this age group perceive and engage with what are presented as some of the most important decisions of their lives (see **Challenge 3: Paralysis**).

I am not going to reinvent a wheel rigorously built by Blakemore and others, but the fundamental lack of experience that young people have to draw on at their most critical moments of decision-making is bound to be a disadvantage. Careers professionals know that experience is a fundamental positive factor in helping people make decisions about their interests, values, environment, and goals, and is central to self-awareness – which itself is highly valued by employers in young, new employees. But it is a vicious circle, because without the experience to draw on – even a sequence of negative experiences ('I don't want to work in an office', 'I don't want to sit at a computer all day', 'I don't want to work on my own') – it is very difficult to know what you do like and want.

The Benchmarks in the statutory guidance that refer to the importance of engaging with workplaces and employees (5 and 6) go some way towards addressing experiences, through observations and conversations at least. But how much experience is enough experience? Are 'encounters' the same as experiences? And is it possible to make any kind of decision about the future if those opportunities are limited, particularly as they are during and after a pandemic? We need to try to answer those questions, because the one thing we cannot do anything about is the neuroscience of the adolescent brain!

Summary

So those are the Challenges:

Challenge 1: The Hourglass Phenomenon

Challenge 2: Qualifications as Knowledge Assets

Challenge 3: Paralysis

Challenge 4: Narrowing definitions of success

Challenge 5: The Neuroscience of the adolescent brain

They look like pretty big ones, because they are tied into some fairly immovable features of national education policy, historically embedded processes, culture and neuroscience. But I genuinely believe – and this is borne out by practical trial and years of experience trying to tackle these challenges and find solutions that learners can engage with – that they are all surmountable right now. It would be brilliant and valuable if policy-makers and politicians would think more constructively about some of the challenges they continually reinforce. But until they do, the following chapters will outline what you can do in your school or college, or your family or community, to enable the learners you know to make better transitions through education into work.

The Environment

So, I have outlined those immovable obstacles that learners face, and it would be easy to feel that Challenges offer nothing but problems. But as the later chapters of this book will show, solutions arise from problems and not simply in opposition to them. I think the same is true when we look a bit more widely at the Environment in which these Challenges are situated:

Environment 1: We need to talk about Employability

Environment 2: Diversity: Human and subject

Environment 3: Mind the gap?

Environment 4: Professionalism and work-readiness

Environment 1: We need to talk about Employability

I have a colleague who suspects that the word 'Employability' must be made up, because the first few times you type it in a word-processing package, it underlines it as an error. Certainly – and far more problematically – learners generally do not encounter this word unless they enter higher education, and they may not even engage with or understand it then. I have been head of two university Careers services which have the word 'Employability' in their titles, and yet colleagues in my own teams were often not clear about what we really meant until I made a focused effort to ensure that they, and everyone else in the university, had a definition that was meaningful to everyone.

One of the reasons for this environmental factor is that Employability means different things to different people:

- To employers, Employability is capture of all the things they are looking for in the people they want to employ, however young or old, and at whatever stage of learning or experience
- To university senior managers, particularly those preoccupied by data of graduate outcomes, Employability is often equated with 'employment' – but they are not the same thing at all
- And those who have written about Employability, mostly in scholarly journals or books about Careers theory, have created a range of summative definitions that never actually make it into learners' worlds.

Furthermore, I do not think this situation has been helped by university Careers services, in particular, having to use those scholarly definitions to justify their activities and functions in a scholarly context. Even universities with Employability strategies are often not really clear about what they mean by Employability, and certainly that messaging often doesn't reach students in a way they can understand and do something with. Employability in higher education becomes a glue that holds strategic and operational decisions together, but rarely enters the student's world in a way they can act on – except through the Careers service.

But the reality is that:

- Even in the absence of a deliberate Career choice, people still get their first job
- What gets them a job is their Employability, so it is an actual 'real-world thing'
- You can have low Career readiness and high Employability and still be very successful (I write from personal experience!)
- Employers speak and recruit in the language of Employability
- But that language is not particularly strongly aligned with the language of education.

In fact, we do not really have a consistent way to talk to school and college learners about any of those points. And neither the statutory guidance nor the Benchmarks address Employability.

This environmental factor is one of the strongest reasons I wrote this book. So later on you will find a way that you can talk to learners about the first three bullet points above, and a way to connect what employers say to how you can talk about Employability within the education context.

Environment 2: Diversity: Human and subject

Diversity – a bit like Employability – is probably one of those words which is more misunderstood than understood, but I have included it here because it captures two features of the employment landscape that have defined and will continue to define learners' journeys into work, particularly as we progress into the Fourth Industrial Revolution.

Firstly, employers and researchers repeatedly emphasise the value of a more diverse workforce. Diverse teams solve problems more quickly and effectively if the different approaches they bring are managed inclusively. And diversity means everything, including gender, ethnicity, identity, neurodiversity and physical diversity, age, socio-economic background, and nationality. The Fourth Industrial Revolution is going to present more complex, more fascinating, and more fundamental problems to be solved and opportunities to innovate and shape, and the more diverse the people involved in that, the better the solutions and innovations will be.

But if we look at individuals, they each bring additional diversity from their education and their experiences. And, as I indicated earlier, if we ask employers what they are looking for in terms of 'routes in' to their companies, the significant majority do not look for learners from specific subjects.[1] That is demonstrably true at higher education level where graduates come from one highly specialised subject that is often unrelated to the role they end up in. And it gives even more emphasis to the need to talk about why and how it is that people actually get their first jobs (see **Environment 1**).

But it is even more true when we look at entry to apprenticeships. The Institute of Student Employers' research paper on apprenticeships published in 2019 recommended that the government 'resist short-sighted calls to restrict access to [higher and degree level] apprenticeships on the basis of prior qualifications'. Furthermore, 'Reducing access based on previous qualifications reduces employers' capacity to find the best person for the job and grow the skills that the economy needs' (pp. 33–34). So diversifying qualifications for entry is not the only solution here, and it is certainly not the simplest. Employers want to see the potential to develop through the ability to learn, Attributes, Skills, and some sense of work-readiness that reflects an understanding of what it is to work. They can provide the rest.

Environment 3: Mind the gap?

There is an abundance of literature and reporting on the Science, Technology, Engineering, and Mathematics (STEM) gap, and very often when people talk about the Skills gap in the UK, they are talking about STEM and digital Skills. There is no doubt that, at the time of writing, such a gap exists. But I think that can be pretty intimidating to a learner who might be presented with the argument laid out in Figure 4, but has some thoughts of their own.

There are a number of hidden potholes in this part of the Environment, so it would be worth picking out two of them before we move on and fall into them.

Firstly, yes, there is considerable growth in the number and range of jobs in STEM and digital-related sectors. But for all that we need people to build algorithms and software, artificial intelligence (AI) requires a human and creative input. This can only be provided by actual humans with emotional, creative, and imaginative capabilities. So STEM and digital roles do not exist in isolation.

Building on that, some of the Attributes and Skills required for STEM and digital roles require the very same Attributes and Skills that are developed in non-STEM subjects. I will dig into this in more detail later, but here are some examples:

- Making non-linear connections – English Literature, Music, Art
- Creativity – all creative and performing arts
- Expressing the same idea in different ways – English Literature, foreign languages

Figure 4. A stressful conversation

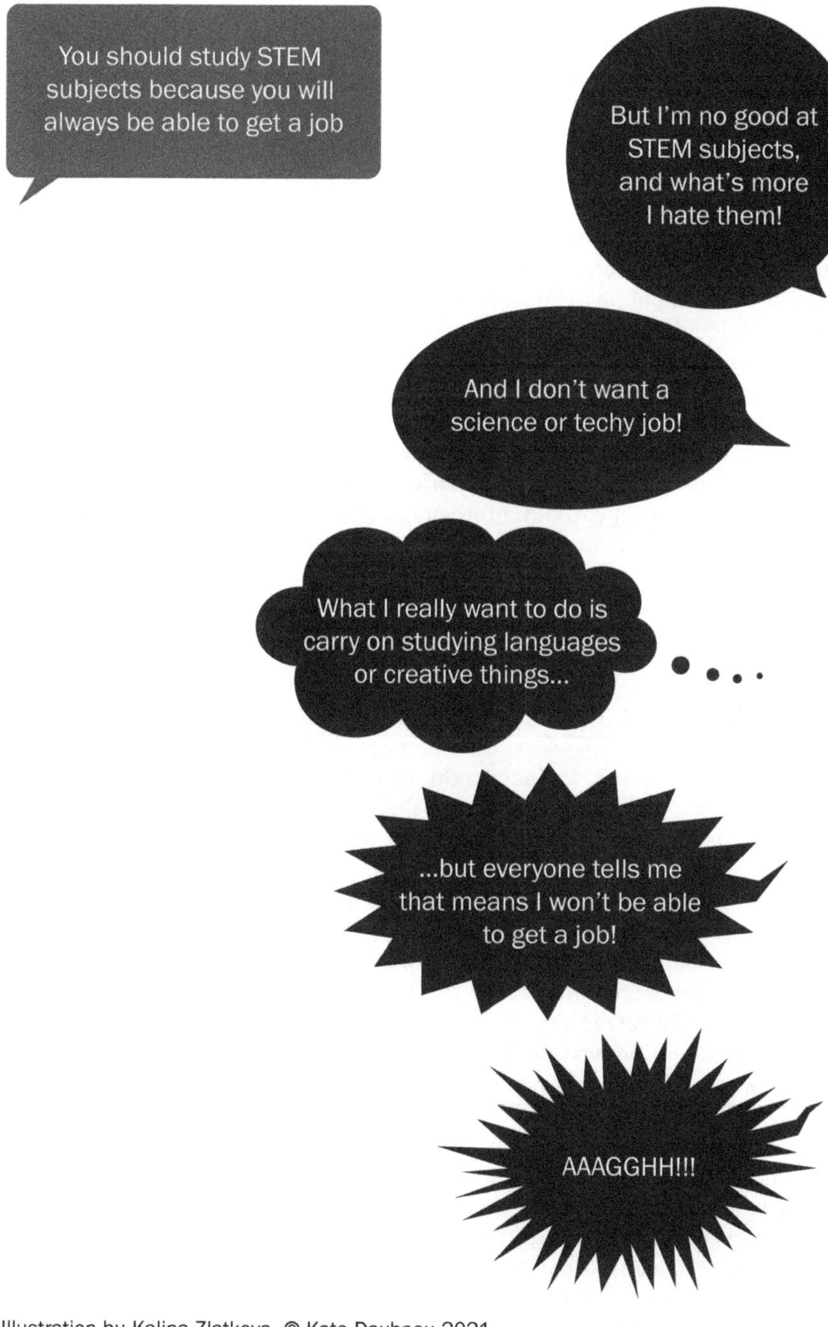

- Attention to detail – History, English Literature, Music, Design, Art, Philosophy
- Finding the causes of things – History
- Making connections – social sciences, English Literature, History
- Modelling ideas and possibilities from evidence – Economics, History, English Literature, Archaeology, Art.

Hopefully you get the idea. But the far bigger problem, which I have seen over and over in my many years of experience working with learners of all ages, and with employers and educational institutions, is that learners do not have the frameworks or language to know how to deal with the examples above. Neither curriculum documentation nor teaching syllabuses give teachers or learners any help in making connections like this across subjects. So how are they supposed to do that for themselves?

Indeed, even the background material from the Careers and Enterprise Company in their Benchmark Toolkits for schools and colleges focuses primarily on STEM in relation to Benchmark 4, Linking Curriculum Learning to Careers. So there is repeated reinforcement of a message that is very difficult for many learners to hear, and may effectively undermine some of their decision-making by apparently reducing their options for a successful Career in the future.

Environment 4: Professionalism and work-readiness

As if choosing a Career, further study, or even their first job was not a big enough challenge, all learners will also face at some point the transition into work. There is rightly some emphasis in the statutory guidance on the importance of encountering workplaces and getting work experience as part of enabling learners to do this more easily. But only a substantial period of time in work – regularly turning up on time, taking responsibility, completing tasks, following instructions, building relationships – will give learners the experience they need to draw on to make this transition effectively and, one hopes, with some sense of reward.

In higher education we talk a lot to students about the importance of commercial awareness, understanding the bigger picture of what drives organisations, distinguishes sectors and industries, what determines roles at different levels. Recruiters expect that and they place quite a high premium on that, which means the student has a lot of responsibility for gaining that insight through research and experiences.

But while employers will naturally have different expectations of school and college leavers, because they are likely to have had less access to experiences of work, they still have expectations of what might seem very basic elements of professionalism and work-readiness: punctuality, dressing appropriately, behaving appropriately, resilience, and confidence. These are what some call life Skills or soft Skills: I have a particular problem with the word 'soft' whenever used with the word 'Skills' because it implies such Skills are somehow less important. Which they are clearly not.

However, whatever Attributes, behaviours, and attitudes we think learners need to make the transition, underpinning any development of these – and any gain that a learner might be able to make from experience observing or participating in work – is self-awareness. If the learner is not able to reflect on what they see, and how it relates to who they are, then the development of professionalism and work-readiness is just like another curriculum. And not every student will engage.

I explore in more detail the transition to work and how to prepare learners in **Part 5: Transitions**.

Note

1   The Institute of Student Employers annually surveys its members, who recruit a significant proportion of the graduates from UK universities. Every year, at least 75–80 per cent state no preference for degree subject for the roles they are recruiting to.

Introducing Careers and Employability

One of the challenges of the statutory guidance, but this is also true of any programme of Careers education, is it can feel like an ever-expanding proliferation of different activities, held together increasingly loosely the more it grows. So one of the key aims of this book is to show you how everything you are doing enables either the learner's Careers journey or their Employability development, or both.

Careers and Employability are different, but connected. The former is more familiar than the latter, but once you get the hang of the latter, you start seeing it everywhere. They can be explored collectively or separately. But they are most effective when they are considered together.

But Careers and Employability are often misunderstood or, as I noted in the Environment section, not understood at all. When working with learners and students, I find this pair of metaphors to work well for introducing them and demonstrating the difference between them.

Firstly, consider the map in Figure 5. When I get a map, I use it to:

- Figure out where I am
- Discover all the places I can get to
- Help me decide which places most interest me
- Learn how to get to my next destination.

Figure 5. The map

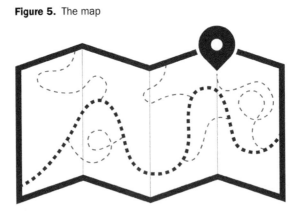

Illustration by Kalina Zlatkova. © Kalina Zlatkova 2021.

So this recognises:

- Journeys
- Personal – my choice
- Bespoke – fitted to me.

It is a great way to describe what 'Careers' is.

Figure 6. The suitcase

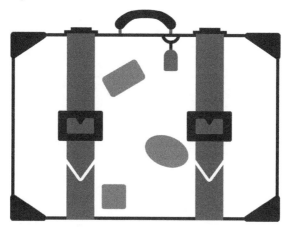

Illustration by Kalina Zlatkova. © Kalina Zlatkova 2021.

Now, consider the suitcase in Figure 6. When I have a suitcase, I can:

- Figure out what I might pick up on my journeys to put in it
- Decide what I need for different journeys
- Put into it the stuff I accumulate along the way
- Remember that everyone always ends up with more in their luggage than they use!

So this recognises:

- Stuff that belongs to me …
- … which is similar to the stuff that everyone else has …
- … but it is my stuff that I gather and take on my journeys.

It is a great way to describe what 'Employability' is.

So in **Part 2** and **Part 3**, we will explore these two words and see what they offer us for enabling learners to move forward.

Part 2

Careers

Figure 5. The map

Illustration by Kalina Zlatkova. © Kalina Zlatkova 2021.

'Careers' is a word that is far more familiar than 'Employability' to pretty much everyone, but it is particularly true for learners up to and beyond higher education. We spend a lot of time in higher education talking about whether we should even use these two words when we work with students, because many learners bring a sense of anxiety or reluctance with them about how to think or talk about their future lives. Students we work with in higher education report that they didn't want to engage with their Careers lessons in school or college, but now they realise they cannot avoid it – and that can pile on the pressure. That is not because Careers Leaders, Careers professionals, and teachers in schools are doing a bad job (far from it!), but it is because of the **Challenges** I outlined earlier.

So, is it better to pretend the elephant is not in the room by calling it something else – a mouse, perhaps? Or is it better to be clear about what it is, so we know exactly what it looks like and it cannot surprise us? As I suggested earlier, this is particularly an issue when we start exploring the word 'Employability' with learners, because they realise it is really important to start getting to grips with it now, but they also fear that they may be somewhere behind where they should be with their Careers thinking.

I think it is essential to be really clear about what these words are and what they mean, why we use them, and why they are important. So, my approach is to keep terminology simple and recognisable, but also to use the words and the metaphors that go with them to show opportunity and not finality.

'Careers' is a really good example of this. It might seem trivial whether it has an 's' on the end or not. But one of the features of the **Paralysis** I talked about earlier is that learners think they are making one choice for life. No wonder they are in a panic! What if they get it wrong? What if they hate it? This is all the **Challenges** rolled into one. And I think that there are times that if we use the word 'Career' instead of 'Careers', or we talk about a single decision or journey, we might subtly reinforce that interpretation.

But talking about multiple Careers makes it a normal outcome. And let's face it, for many of us reading this book (and certainly for me) that is true, because we haven't had one job for our whole lives. We have tried different things out, changed our minds, been promoted, moved employers. As I will explore shortly, when we dig down into Careers a bit more, we go on a new journey each time. So, actually flagging up that plural, and reassuring learners that they are just deciding their next step and not making a decision for always-and-forever, is a really significant benefit of using the word 'Careers' instead of 'Career'. That is something you can and should talk to learners about.

One of the biggest problems often created by a school Careers programme is a surfeit of excellent activity that apparently has less impact than it should. I have met many Careers Leaders, Careers professionals, and teachers who know objectively that what they offer learners is good, who are meeting the Benchmarks if required, and are getting external validation of the quality of their provision. But still they are finding that:

- Learners are slow to engage and realise the value of the provision
- Learners still feel paralysed by choice
- Learners still choose the same narrow outcomes, many of which may not be the right choice for them but they feel is their only choice
- Learners make poor but well-meaning choices because they do not have all the information about themselves that they need.

I want to stress that last point in particular, because I think it is the element most out of reach for Careers Leaders, Careers professionals, and teachers. You will be aware that the most expensive type of provision to learners in terms of time and money is one-to-one guidance. And you will likely know, as well as I do, that you will never be able to give enough resource for every learner to have as much of that as they need.

But that would be to overlook the part that the learner plays in their own guidance and their own Career journeys. We currently reinforce a model that presupposes that the only way a learner can make progress on their journeys is with the guidance of a Careers professional. But, firstly, that cannot be true because billions of people, including you reading this book, have made very successful lifelong Career journeys without having a Careers professional at their side all the way. And, secondly, if we insist that is true while learners are in school, college, and higher education, they are in for a dramatic moment of separation when they reach work, when that kind of support is no longer available to them.

So, what you will see in the coming pages is a set of suggestions that enables learners to adjust quickly to the role they play in their own guidance and their own Career journeys. Because if we can do a better job of enabling learners to get the information about themselves that they need to make decisions, we will see more impact from all the work we are putting in and the other interactions learners have. I think doing that successfully is about focusing on four main themes:

- Giving learners reference points for their Career journeys
- Making sure what you offer is fit for those journeys and not just the Benchmarks or other external parameters
- Giving learners ways to assess their progress on their journeys
- Gathering data about how they are progressing on their journeys.

Careers: The Three Stage Journey

You've got a friend coming round for a chat, and they call you. 'I'm lost. I can't find where you live!' The first thing you ask is, 'Where are you now?' This is why Careers journeys are like maps. It is much easier to get to where you want to get to, if you know where you are starting from.

Many of you will be aware of the cyclic models and theories that exist to describe reflective Careers learning, and will have trained as Careers professionals by developing an understanding of how to use them with clients. Like many Careers theories though, sometimes they are more useful to the practitioner than the learner, and my key aim as a Careers professional has always been to think like the learner. So, the Three Stage Journey I use throughout this book is a snapshot of progression within those theoretically defined cycles, just one phase of the longer iterative Careers journey we all go on. There is no expectation that the student or learner will move through it in a linear fashion, and while they are in your care at school and college, they might go through that journey at least twice, pre-16 and post-16. Furthermore, as I discuss later, movement back and forward between the stages on any one journey is a very natural part of good Careers decision-making.

So, this Three Stage Journey is a useful and consistent way of presenting to the student or learner for the first time the idea that they are progressing through their decision-making towards what happens next, through their own eyes and their own experience. I built the journey in three clear and different stages:

- I'm uncertain about who I might become and what's out there for me
- I've got some ideas but I need to explore more to decide what's right for me
- I understand myself well and have a plan to put into action for my next step.

We all go through these three stages repeatedly throughout our working lives, but for learners up to their early twenties, it might be the first time they have had the journey spelled out for them this way. In this book, I am going to call that Three Stage Journey:

Explore – Encounter – Embark

There is an expression to describe this journey: Career readiness. In other words, the journey to become ready for the next stage of your Career.

I mentioned work-readiness earlier, which reflects the mindset and Career management Skills to be ready to enter the workplace. But Career readiness is a broader concept which concerns the process of self-exploration and choosing what to do next, and requires sound processes of decision-making and self-awareness.[1] It is very widely used in UK higher education, though less so in schools and colleges. I do not think you need to label the Three Stage Journey as 'Career readiness' to be effective in deploying the journey, but if you explain arriving in the final stage as indicating readiness to get started on the next step the learner has chosen, then that can be helpful to them.

Capturing and articulating the journey in this simple way do not just introduce learners to the idea of a journey. It also addresses something which should not be an issue, but often is. Every university has a wide demographic of students, whether internationally or domestically, of different ages and backgrounds and study interests. With that diversity, you can be sure that students' understanding of what Careers activities are for is equally diverse and, sadly, often incomplete. University Careers services are sometimes guilty of presenting activities to students with the confidence that they are offering a great range with great value. But that is often founded on the assumption that the student will know why those activities are valuable.

But if you 'think like the student', you quickly realise that is not equally true for every student. So, it is essential that students and learners understand the value of a Careers activity *in relation to who they are and where they are on their journey*, and not solely in abstract. A good example of why this is important emerges when you consider the following statement:

> One-to-one guidance is the heart of great Careers provision.

But one-to-one guidance is not equally valuable to every learner because its value to the learner depends on where they are on their journey. A learner who has made a decision about their next step and is clear about their plan of action might need advice and information about where to get a particular insight, while a learner who feels clueless about their future really does need guidance to help explore their options for the first time. So, for a learner in the Explore stage, that statement might be true. But for a learner in the Embark stage, that is not as true as, say, interactions with employers.

There are lots of other good reasons for applying this Three Stage Journey that will become apparent in the coming sections. But the key point is this – whatever you call it, this Three Stage Journey generates a lot of possible ways for learners to engage, find themselves, and move themselves forward. And from your point of view as a Careers Leader, Careers professional, or teacher, framing all your activity like this will help learners get far more impact from what you are doing for and with them. Your goal is to help them move forward on their Career journeys.

But there is another really key function and benefit of this Three Stage Journey: to you as the person planning and delivering the work. I mentioned above that you are already delivering content, and it is probably good quality, well thought out, and bringing together a range of input from external perspectives. But I imagine that you, like me, are very keen to open up new ways to get far more value from what we do with and for our learners or students at each of those stages.

So, with that in mind, in this section of the book I am going to introduce a wheel of activities (Figure 7) to engage learners in a fresh way that you should be able to do without too much additional time and resource. Where you do need to devote time, you should only have to do it once and then it is done in a way that should have lasting impact. You do not need to do everything on the wheel, but the more you do, the more cumulative benefit you should see from across your existing programme.

It makes most sense to do the activities in order, because they build on each other. However, you do not have to do all of them, but if you are doing

Figure 7. Explore Encounter Embark activity wheel

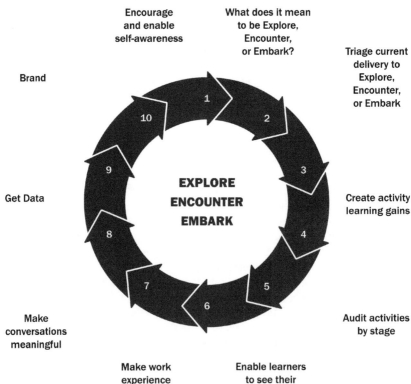

Illustration by Kalina Zlatkova. Wheel design © Kalina Zlatkova 2021. Concept © Kate Daubney 2021.

Activity 3, I suggest thinking about whether you can do **4** and **5** as well, because if done together, they will create significant impact for learners.

For each activity I will start with some explanation. Then I summarise the **Key principles** for you, some simple **Messages for learners**, and then some **Actions** you can take. I finish up by putting the activity in the **Context** of the statutory guidance Benchmarks, for those who have to follow them. I also summarise all the messages for learners at the end of **Part 2**.

Note

1 It is worth noting that at the time of writing (2021), North American Careers professionals use Career readiness to mean something slightly different, which is closer to what I call Employability. Just something to bear in mind if you are reading around the subject.

Activity 1: Encourage and enable self-awareness

I noted earlier that Careers journeys are like maps. It is much easier to get to where you want to get to, if you know where you are starting from. So, as I have suggested earlier in this book, self-awareness is fundamental for all of us to knowing where we are, and therefore to making good Careers decisions.

It is particularly important for learners making their first decisions, not least because they might complete the decision-making cycle several times in just a few years: subjects studied to 15 or 16 years old; then work choices or subjects studied to 17 or 18; then work choices or subjects studied in higher education … and on beyond that. This is core to **Challenge 1: The Hourglass Phenomenon** and **Challenge 3: Paralysis**.

But instead of seeing these decisions only as time-specific hurdles to be overcome, you can strongly support and enable learners to make these decisions more calmly and confidently by turning that perception around. If you start instead with the idea that learners are on a sequence of short journeys in which these decisions play a part, and at all times they know where they are on their journey, then it becomes less about deadlines and more about progress through that journey. Each time a stage is completed, a new journey begins. And sometimes, in fact increasingly as we move through our Careers, the journey does not start again at the beginning (Explore), but halfway through (Encounter).

I think that last point is really important to keep Careers education inclusive for all. We have all worked with learners who seem to know exactly where they are heading with unwavering clarity. And we've also worked with many learners who seem adrift, appear to be slow or unwilling to engage with their futures, and are put off by the clarity of their peers. As I outlined in the **Challenges** section, there are many really good reasons for it and it is essential that those latter learners do not feel undermined or disempowered. So **Activity 1** is not about forcing more of the undecideds into certainty. It is about giving every learner a sense of where they are on their journey so they can find their way towards certainty more easily.

I think it is also important to encourage learners that it is perfectly possible to make all sorts of 'deadline decisions', particularly about subject choices, without necessarily making progress on a Career journey. Exams taken at 15 or 16 years old shouldn't be positioned as framing a lifelong commitment to one Career outcome. They should be presented as one element in keeping options open. The only caveat is that if a subject is dropped at that stage but needed later, some journeys might take longer. For example, dropping Chemistry at 16 might make a Career in veterinary, food, or medical sciences take a bit longer. But that should not, in my opinion, be framed as a bad decision. It is like travelling from Glasgow to London via Cardiff. It is not the most direct route, but the journey can still be valuable and interesting in itself. And you will still get from Glasgow to London.

So, **Activity 1** is about defining the journey for your learners. To remind you, this is how I describe Explore Encounter Embark:

- **Explore:** I'm uncertain about who I might become and what's out there for me
- **Encounter:** I've got some ideas but I need to explore more to decide what's right for me
- **Embark:** I understand myself well and have a plan to put into action for my next step.

Key principles for you

In developing Explore Encounter Embark to describe the journey, I stuck to some simple principles that encourage and enable self-awareness:

1 *Three stages keeps it simple for learners.* Any more than three quickly feels overwhelming; and fewer than three gives you a start and a finish, but no transition phase from one to the other.

2 *Clear but inclusive language is important.* In higher education, some Careers services use words like 'Compete' instead of 'Embark'. But if you want to set up your own business, 'Compete' doesn't make as much sense. Others use Decide rather than Explore, but I feel that the first stage should be more about exploration than conclusion. Whatever words you choose, language that includes diverse starting and finishing points, and is more about the journey than the outcome is likely to be more impactful and enduring.

3 *Consistency is essential: Choose your language and stick to it for everything.* We like to think up jazzy names for stuff to get learners engaged, but the reality is that less is more in this context. Making activities recognisable in the context of the journey is what gets learners engaged and gives it meaning. So, keep it simple and make sure it does what it says on the label.

Messages for learners

And with those key principles for you come simple messages you can share with learners:

Where am I right now? Which statement applies best to me?

It doesn't matter where I start on my journey

If I don't know how to get to where I want to get to yet, at least I know where I am now, and I can discover some journeys from here

There's no such thing as a bad decision; it might just take me longer to get to my destination if I take a route that I later decide wasn't quite right for me.

Actions

- Choose the labels for your Three Stage Journey; there are some suggestions in Appendix 2.

Context value

In doing this, you are addressing the needs of each learner (Benchmark 3) because every learner can see themselves in the language of the Career journey. Putting the journey first immediately brings the learner into everything you do, because their entry point is themselves and not the activities you are offering.

Activity 2: What does it mean to be Explore, Encounter, or Embark?

Labelling phases is not enough on its own. I hope it will always be clear what Explore, Encounter, and Embark mean to any learners who see it because I chose clear, unambiguous words. But using some simple, consistent explanations for those three stages on the journey is essential to ensure inclusion and avoid confusion.

In developing a Three Stage Careers Journey, I wanted students to understand what their journey looked like through three main lenses: their Careers journeys, their Employability development, and the Bigger Picture. As I discussed in the **Environment** section, successful outcomes for learners rely on good Careers decision-making, an understanding of their own Employability, and an awareness of the world that they are moving into. So, in Figure 8 you can see statements that capture the three stages of the journey through each of those lenses.

There is a lot to read and process here! Working with Careers Leaders, Careers professionals, and teachers, I know they have found it really useful to see the whole journey through the three lenses presented together. But it can be a lot for learners to take in, depending on where they are on their journeys. So here are some thoughts about how you might use this grid.

- It will not always be helpful to present the complete grid because for some learners, particularly those in Explore at their earliest decision-making phase, this would be quite off-putting! Sometimes one stage (e.g. Careers/Explore) will give you all you need to start a discussion.
- I have found it can be helpful to separate out Employability development from Careers learning, because a student might develop their Employability assets at a different pace than their Careers decision-making. I talk about that in more detail in the second half of this book.
- When you first present the journey to learners, you could use only the Careers statements, as in Figure 9.
- Or you could consolidate Careers, Employability, and the Bigger Picture statements into one, as in Figure 10.

A key point to consider now, which I raised earlier, is that while this is presented as a linear journey, most learners will not make it in a linear fashion.

Figure 8. Explore Encounter Embark: The complete journey

	EXPLORE	ENCOUNTER	EMBARK
CAREERS: Who am I and where am I going?	I'm uncertain about who I might become and what's out there for me	I've got some ideas but I need to explore more to decide what's right for me	I understand myself well and have a plan to put into action
EMPLOYABILITY: What do I need to get me there?	I'm not aware of what I have to offer, or how my qualifications are going to help with my future	I'm beginning to understand how my knowledge, attributes, skills and experience support my future options and what I might need to develop	I'm confident in identifying what knowledge, attributes, skills and experience I have developed through what I study and do, articulating what is relevant
THE BIGGER PICTURE: What is the working world I am going to enter?	What does the working world expect of me in the Career of my choice?	How can information and experiences help me become successful and employment-ready in the Careers that interest me?	I can analyse and apply relevant information to achieve my Career choice and be successful in it

Table design by Kalina Zlatkova. © Kate Daubney 2021.

Figure 9. Explore Encounter Embark: The Careers statements

Table design by Kalina Zlatkova. © Kate Daubney 2021.

Figure 10. Explore Encounter Embark: The combined statements

Table design by Kalina Zlatkova. © Kate Daubney 2021.

They are very likely to circle around between Explore and Encounter for a while, and perhaps even get as far as Embark where they might make a decision and then change their minds and go back to Encounter or even to Explore. This is one of the reasons I talk about multiple Careers journeys.

You will be familiar with this already, and it is important to emphasise to learners that this circularity and uncertainty are normal and welcome. It all underpins better self-awareness, and the value in that uncertainty is derived from awareness of it. Enabling a learner to keep track of why they changed their mind, why they felt unsure, and how it has or will enable them to make progress again are all helpful. Self-identifying where they are is a key part of keeping track of the journeys and maintaining confidence in themselves.

Key principles for you

1 *First person language works best.* If we 'think like the learner' rather than as the Careers professional or teacher, then it is sensible to use the language learners would use to describe themselves. So, use 'I' instead of 'You'. It also feels less directive and encourages the learner to own their journey instead of feeling pushed along it by someone else.

2 *Keep explanations simple.* Sum it up in one sentence because learners are more likely to read the whole thing!

3 *Use these statements as starting points for conversations with learners.* A learner will get more impact from a conversation if they can see how it

relates to where they are. Guidance can sometimes feel to the learner like they are being asked to leap to a final choice ('What do you want to do?'), whereas a conversation that starts with the learner noticing where they are on their journey will immediately be a conversation that the learner owns and leads.

Messages for learners

Where am I right now? Which statement applies best to me?

It doesn't matter where I start on my journey

If I don't know how to get to where I want to get to yet, at least I know where I am now, and I can plan my journey from here

There's no such thing as a bad decision; it might just take me longer to get to my destination if I take a route that I later decide wasn't quite right for me

Moving backwards is sometimes as useful as moving forward, because I am always learning something.

Actions

- Write a statement for each of your journey stage words in the first person that describes what the learner feels like at that stage
  - ○ You can involve learners in this as an activity if you want to, as part of introducing personal guidance
  - ○ You can use this as an activity for analysing Careers stories from alumni, parents, or famous people. Where do the decisions they made sit on their Three Stage Careers Journey?

Context value

As with **Activity 1**, in doing this you are addressing the needs of each learner (Benchmark 3) because every learner can see themselves in the language of the Career journey. Putting the journey first immediately brings the learner into everything you do, because again their entry point is themselves and not the activities you are offering.

You are also building the foundation for personal guidance (Benchmark 8) because a learner who has an idea of where they are when they start a guidance conversation is going to get much more out of it.

Activity 3: Triage current delivery to Explore Encounter Embark

[Activities 3, 4 and 5 go together; you will get more impact out of Activity 3 if you can do 4 and 5 as well. But if you can only do one activity, do Activity 3. If you can only do two, do Activities 3 and 4.]

I mentioned earlier that higher education Careers services often – and rightly – are confident that they are offering good activities to students. And if you have had your Careers programme peer-reviewed or externally assessed, you probably feel the same way. But, as I suggested, there is a gulf in understanding, experience, and expertise between what we know as Careers Leaders, Careers professionals, and teachers, and how learners experience things. And if we remember **Challenge 5: The Neuroscience of the adolescent brain**, we know that learners in school, college, and higher education often do not have the experiences to draw on to make sense of what is on offer to them.

So, a key step I took to get more value out of the Three Stage Journey I built was to see how the services we offered aligned with those three stages. I didn't think it was enough to expect students to guess for themselves whether, for example, a guidance appointment was useful to them or not, particularly if they had never used such a service before.

Making this evaluation gave me quite a shock too: there is a perception by outsiders to the Careers world that our main value is in giving CV advice. This often makes Careers professionals very irritated because much of our expertise and excellence is in the guidance and exploration activities; CVs are really the last step on the journey. But when I looked at how our service activities spread across the three stages of our journey, I realised how much of what we offered sat in the final phase. I do not think this is true of only our Careers service, but it would explain partly why people have that perception of what Careers services do.

For example, among our dozens of different activities for students, we offered these:

- Alumni speed-meets
- Employer panel events

- Research internships
- Careers guidance appointments
- Interview practice
- Employer-led skill development sessions
- Careers fairs by employment sector.

If you are a student, how do you know which of these you are supposed to go to? You can read the event or activity description, but you still have to figure out whether it is useful to you. And if it is hard to do that, or you still cannot figure out what it is for, then you are not likely to engage.

But what if we divided the activities up by journey stage?

Figure 11. Explore Encounter Embark: Distribution of Careers activities by stage

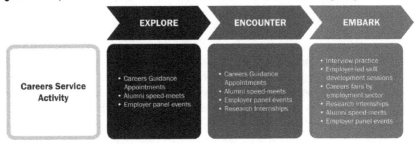

Table design by Kalina Zlatkova. © Kate Daubney 2021.

You can see that most of these activities end up in more than one phase. In fact, that is a good thing, because you want things you offer to be meaningful to as many learners as possible. And the key to making that happen is to ensure learners understand how an activity is meaningful to them for their journey stage (we will cover that in **Activity 4**). You can see, for example, that Careers guidance appointments are not really for Embark stage students; they get application advice appointments instead because guidance is most impactful for those who are Exploring and Encountering.

So, a triage process like this means that the learner can immediately identify which activities are there for them at their journey stage. And when you are building your Careers programme, you can immediately see the gaps (more on that in **Activity 5**).

So, if we now look at some of the activities you offer in your learning environment, you might consider:

- Employer visits
- FE/HE visits
- Talks
- School fairs
- Parent/alumni talks

- One-to-ones
- Profiling tools
- Information and websites
- Tutor conversations.

How would you divide those up across Explore Encounter Embark?

As with my triage above, activities that involve more direct reflection for the learner, for example, are more likely to be useful in Explore and Encounter. It is also worth thinking about the impact of using tools and platforms where you do not have much or any control over the content: learners need support to know how such tools are meant to help them, so aligning activities with journey stages is really useful.

Key principles for you

1 *Ask yourself honestly which journey stages an activity is most impactful for.* The Benchmarks aren't written like this, but those regarding employers and workplaces are generally most valuable for learners in Encounter and Embark who need to imagine themselves in a future outcome, while those regarding labour market information, individual needs, and guidance are more useful to learners in Explore and Encounter.

2 *Put yourself in the learner's shoes: 'If I am feeling clueless about what I want from my future, or I haven't had any kind of Careers interaction before, will I immediately understand what this activity is for?'* Careers activities often take a huge amount of time and effort to organise and implement, and it can be frustrating to find out something is not as useful as you hoped it would be, particularly if other people are involved. But thinking about the usefulness of an activity to learners in relation to their Careers journey stage is essential if you are to capture the real value.

Messages for learners

There are activities for me, whatever stage of my journey I am at

Different activities are useful at different stages

I might find the same activity useful in different ways at different stages on my Career journeys.

Actions

- Make a list of all your activities across the whole of your school or college, include platforms, resources, future and past activities
- Label each activity by learner stage; if an activity sits in multiple stages, start thinking about how its value to the learner differs between Explore, Encounter and Embark

- **Activities 4** and **5** will help you get the most value from this activity if you can do them too.

Context value

In doing this activity, you are building the foundations for a stable Careers programme (Benchmark 1) that actually addresses the needs of each learner (Benchmark 3). And in conjunction with **Activity 5**, you will end up with a comprehensive programme that supports learners at all stages of their journey. You are also maximising the benefits of information and engagement activities (Benchmarks 2, 5, 6, 7, 8) because the learner can see where those types of activity fit with their journey.

Activity 4: Create activity learning gains

Good Careers provision is all about answering this question from the learner:

What will change for me as a result of doing/reading/engaging with this?

I have made this point several times now, but it is really unhelpful to learners to assume that they know what the point of different Careers activities and resources is. Some will work it out, some will have external reference points that help them identify and gain value, some will have someone to explain it to them. But we cannot and should not assume any of those are true for anyone. So, assume it is true for no-one and start from there.

Good teaching and learning principles tell us that being clear about learning outcomes is fundamental to enabling learners to maximise their benefit. And there is no reason why this should not also be applied to Careers education too. A note here: I call them learning 'gains' rather than 'outcomes'. I feel an outcome is something that happens to you, whereas a gain can be achieved by and therefore owned by the learner.

Key principles for you

I am putting the principles in early in this section, because they help explain why articulating learning gain is so important:

1 *Learning gains should differentiate by stage of Career journey, just as learning outcomes would by level of study in an academic subject*
2 *Like the learning journey stages, use the first person so that the learner hears the statements in their own voice*
3 *Writing a learning gain helps you figure out if the activity is actually going to make a difference to the learner's Career journey*
4 *Writing a learning gain helps you figure out what needs to be added to an event or resource to help the learner gain the value either during or after*
5 *Learning gains frame expectations of value for the learner, and indicate that the learner should expect some benefit and a change of Career readiness, however small*
6 *Learning gains should enable the learner to leave the activity being confident that 'I now know something I didn't know before and what that means to me and my Career journey'*

7   *Learning gains provide great conversation openers*: 'What do you now know that you didn't know before you did/read/went to this?' 'What does that mean to you and why is it important/valuable to you?'

Creating learning gains is much easier for some kinds of activity than others. Figure 12 shows some you might use for a Careers guidance appointment:

Figure 12. Explore Encounter Embark: Sample learning gains for a guidance appointment

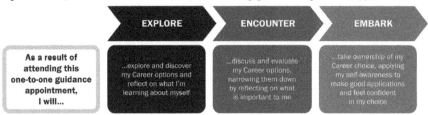

Table design by Kalina Zlatkova. © Kate Daubney 2021.

But it can be harder to create them for labour market information websites or university prospectuses. Information, in particular, very often needs more triage and explanation than other kinds of activities, because as a passive resource, it does not react and respond to the learner. So, a good set of learning gains for information sources might combine Careers learning and bigger picture landscape understanding (see Figure 13).

Figure 13. Explore Encounter Embark: Sample learning gains for information resources

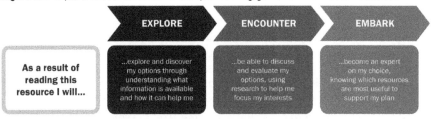

Table design by Kalina Zlatkova. © Kate Daubney 2021.

Fundamental to all these learning gains is the need to encourage learners that everyone, no matter where they are on their journey, can take something away from an activity. Although in **Activity 3**, we saw that some Careers interventions are more useful at some journey stages than others, we want to encourage all learners to find value in everything we offer, so it is a good idea to write learning gains for each activity that describe the gains at each of the three stages, so that activities look and are experienced as inclusive to all.

It can also be really useful to share these learning gains and your Three Stage Journey with any visiting speakers or employers. Briefing visitors that there are learners at different stages in the audience – particularly those all in the same year group – will help them think about what information to share, and how, for learners at each stage. For example, higher education Careers services often find that employers attending Careers fairs at university campuses are expecting to meet students who are in their final stages of Career planning. But the reality is that students in earlier stages of Career readiness find such events are a great way to get a more informal feel for what a job or sector might be like. It is our role as the Careers service to manage expectations on both sides, but I never want to turn a learner away. So, the learning gains are a simple and easy way to say to everyone: 'There is something here for you.'

No matter how much or how little content you have in your programme, creating learning gains for what you already deliver will help your learners get more value from what you are already delivering. Enabling learners to recognise themselves and their needs in the learning gains increases the likelihood of your existing interventions making the difference you want them to make.

Messages for learners

There are activities for me, whatever stage of my journey I am at

I know what will change for me as a result of doing/reading/engaging with this

If I know where I am on my journey, I can be sure how each activity will help me progress on my journey

I will find the same activity useful in different ways at different stages on my journey.

Actions

- Create simple learning gains for each of the three stages, for each category of Careers programme activity you offer
  - You might choose to categorise activities as one-to-ones, group learning, events, information, or experiences, for example, or in any other way that makes sense for your programme
  - Creating summary learning gains in each category for your three journey stages means that if you do lots of different events, for example, you have a universal learning gain set to start with
- Once you have written your category learning gains, for example, for all your events, you can create different learning gains for activities in the same category which are different, e.g. visits to employers and visits to FE/HE
- Consider how you are going to help learners navigate information resources and platforms

    ◦ For example, if you create your own sector sheets (e.g. Careers in Health), you could show how different websites and resources align to different journey stages, e.g. *Prospects* for Explore, a professional body website for Embark.

Context value

By creating learning gains, you are maximising the benefits of your Careers programme (Benchmark 1) because the learning gains actually address the needs of each learner (Benchmark 3). You can then write new learning gains as you create any new programme elements, after **Activity 5**. You are also maximising the benefits of information and engagement activities (Benchmarks 2, 5, 6, 7, 8) because the learner can see how and why every activity enables them to progress on their journey.

Activity 5: Audit your activities across your journey stages

Building on **Activity 3**, an audit helps you to see where there are gaps in your provision by journey stage. As I noted earlier, when we first did an audit of our workshops and group learning in our Careers service, I realised how much of it was centred on the final stage (CV workshops, application processes, interview Skills, assessment centres) and how little on the exploratory stages. We were delivering more content in the area where less specialist expertise was required, while the majority of our excellence as Careers professionals was in guidance and reflection – starting students off on their journey of self-discovery – but we had no group learning there.

Learners generally need more content and activities to help them through Explore and Encounter; to some extent, the Benchmarks recognise that by noting the importance of addressing the needs of each pupil and personal guidance (Benchmarks 3 and 8). However, there is a massive amount of value that can be added through group learning and online learning in Explore and Encounter, so if you see you have gaps in those stages, do not think that your only solution is to do more one-to-one guidance. Group learning gives you the opportunity for peer learning and reflection: sometimes learners are more prepared to tell each other something than they are to tell a Careers professional or teacher. Likewise, online learning can give learners a more personal space in which to reflect and explore their thoughts before sharing.

You can develop some really effective reflective content on e-learning platforms that focuses on the core elements of interests and values in decision-making, and will get learners started on their reflective journey before they have a personal guidance session. The pandemic has forced all our education onto digital platforms, but Careers engagement in higher education increased when delivered as blended combinations of online learning and virtual workshops. So, e-learning can be a really powerful tool as a springboard for engaging those with low Career readiness who are perhaps cautious about engaging for the first time, particularly in front of peers and friends. Likewise, if you use profiling tools,[1] then some post-results reflection and further research can be a good way for the learner to take control of their self-discovery.

Other content you can develop might include 'how-to' guides that look at progressing decision-making by narrowing choices. These are particularly useful for Encounter stages, such as:

- How to choose A level/Higher/University subjects
- How to choose a useful work experience
- How to choose the right university for me
- How to choose an apprenticeship sector.

For example, it is no good having a UCAS application form workshop at the Embark stage if you have learners in the room who have not yet figured out what subject they want to do. Likewise, there are thousands of apprenticeships, so an Encounter learner who knows they want to do an apprenticeship might still need help choosing the right sector and the right experience.

The greatest value you can bring to learners is to get them from Explore to Encounter, and Encounter to Embark. As I noted earlier, learners who have a plan when they leave an educational stage are more likely to achieve it, go on and be successful, and will probably establish good habits for the future. So, if you do not have capacity or resource to create any new activities or events, think about how you can create and use learning gains to help learners get more value at the Explore and Encounter stages from what you already do.

Key principles for you

1 *When you see gaps in provision, don't panic!* Is it really a gap, or can it be covered by making learning gains clearer for existing activities? Adding something new is not always the best or only solution.
2 *Gaps are not always a sign that there is something missing in the programme for all learners.* With more learners in Explore, one employer event or alumni/parent talks can create a huge range of learning gain in Explore and Encounter, rather than in Embark: think about what you can do with pre- and post-reflection for learners, and with good advance briefing for speakers and visitors.

   Likewise, if your learner demographic is more skewed towards high-achieving university destinations, then you may need fewer, more specific resources in Explore. You may have fewer Explore learners, but they may need more bespoke provision to discover choices that are different from the majority.
3 *If you do not have capacity to create new activities in gap areas, use your learning gains to make the value of existing activities more clear to learners.* The resource you offer as a Careers Leader, Careers professional, or teacher may be best spent in building good infrastructure for navigation and explanation, rather than in creating lots of new activities.

Messages for learners

There are activities for me, whatever stage of my journey I am at

I know what will change for me as a result of doing/reading/engaging with this

If I know where I am on my journey, I can be sure how each activity will help me progress on my journey

I will find the same activity useful in different ways at different stages on my journey

Moving from Explore to Encounter, or Encounter to Embark will be really useful for me, because I will learn how to make decisions well about what I want to do.

Actions

- Review your **Activity 3** triage of activities by journey stage and look for any gaps, particularly in Explore and Encounter
- Are the gaps genuinely an issue for the learner demographic you have?
- If you have gaps, determine whether you really need any new activities – and whether you have capacity or resource to develop any
- Review the learning gains for your existing activities, both in the same journey stage and in the later ones; can you do more with these to generate learning where you seem to have gaps?

Context value

By auditing your activities against learning journey stages, you are ensuring your Careers programme doesn't just meet the Benchmarks (if you are required to) but also addresses the needs of each learner (Benchmarks 1 and 3). Reflecting on how learning gains can help fill gaps will help you maximise the benefits of information and engagement activities (Benchmarks 2, 5, 6, 7, 8) because the learner can see how and why every activity enables them to progress on their journey.

Note

1 I am personally not a fan of profiling tools because I think they can pigeonhole choices too early and narrow learners' views of what they are suited to. I'm also concerned that learners are led to believe that their interests and their Skills and aptitudes are fixed, and can never change. If you are using these tools, then set tasks afterwards that encourage more exploration and reflection beyond the 'answers' the tools generate, and get learners to reflect with their peers on what it would be like to try very different choices to the ones that appear in their results, for example 'agricultural engineer' instead of 'data scientist', or 'lab technician' and 'theatre technician'. This will help keep horizons broader and enable learners to engage with the results, and not just accept them without question or challenge.

Activity 6: Enable learners to see their learning gain

What will change for me as a result of doing/reading/engaging with this?

As I outlined in **Activities 4** and **5**, helping learners answer this key question is essential to them making progress on their Careers journeys. But as educators, you know the vital part that reflection plays in learning. We can already achieve a lot by establishing a Careers journey in stages, organising activities by stage, and adding learning gains. But even though the learner cannot avoid engaging with these by virtue of their very presence, the reality is that they need a way to constantly reflect and bring that learning back to themselves.

It would also be unrealistic to assume that in just two interventions a learner can leap from Explore to Embark. These journeys take time and, as I suggested earlier, backwards movement is not only possible but likely and also welcome. If you have studied any of the Careers models, you will know that iteration – going round and round on a reflective cycle – is a key element to successful Careers learning. And sometimes that includes retracing your steps to see where you might have got distracted or diverted or made an assumption or leap. In **Activity 9**, I explore gathering and using data, but I would discourage you from any kind of league table thinking about Careers journeys. Yes, ideally, we want learners to leave an educational stage with a clear idea and plan for what they are going to do next. But the neuroscience in **Challenge 5** tells us that is tricky and ambitious and is – I would suggest – possibly unrealistic for many learners.

But we do want to enable learners to know where they are and which way they should be heading. This self-awareness is your definition of success. Part of that means that a learner answering the question above not only can tell you where they were before they did/read/engaged with the activity, but also what has changed for them. They might not have moved on (or backwards) in journey stages, but they can tell you what they know now, particularly about themselves. So we need to make that happen in any way we can.

So, a key element to embedding successfully the Three Stage Journey is to introduce a very short reflective survey after key activities. You might identify one-to-ones and groupwork, for example, as activities which are likely to have the most influence on Careers journey progress. To underpin awareness of that progress, therefore, we need to create that awareness in the first place: we simply ask learners to identify their Careers journey stage before the activity and after. The process of stopping and asking themselves, 'What has changed?

Where am I now?' is so valuable. Just like formative assessment, we are putting down markers for how their learning is changing.

For example, you could use this example for any activity, including a one-to-one guidance conversation:

Before I attended this personal guidance appointment:

- I felt uncertain about who I might become and what's out there for me
- I had some ideas about what I want to do next, but needed help narrowing them down
- I had a really clear idea of what I want to do next.

After attending this personal guidance appointment:

- I still feel uncertain about who I might become, but I know how to start thinking about it
- I have started to narrow my ideas down and know what other information and experiences I need to access to help me do that
- I now know what I want to do and what steps I need to take next.

The wording here in the *After* answers is designed to ensure that a learner who remains in the same stage after the interaction is still encouraged that something should and probably will have changed for them. We want to reassure them that, for example, it is not something to worry about if they still feel uncertain, but they should have left with some ideas about what to do next and the prospect of movement to the next stage is now more present than it was before. In Careers education we emphasise the importance of the learner or student identifying and taking ownership of their next steps. So, these phrases in the *After* answers also indicate that the learner is the person who will start those next steps themselves.

As with the Career readiness questions, an interesting consideration is whether you should use the Careers journey stage words or not. I do not think there is a right answer here, and it depends on whether you are looking to embed the stage words with everything you do in your programme, or want to place more emphasis on the experience and self-description of what it is to be in the stage. This is particularly important in the *After* statements, where we want to encourage a learner that something has changed, even if they have not changed journey stage.

Your school or college's virtual learning environment or management system may give you a digital tool to ask questions for this purpose, or you can do it instantly by asking the learner the question at the end of an interaction. However you approach this intentional reflection opportunity though, it is the constant, consistent, and coherent iteration of the same marker points for the Careers journey which learners benefit from to develop their self-awareness. In the **Actions** section below, I suggest some different ways to achieve this.

Key principles for you

1 *Reflection is the best way to cement learning gain and answer the question, 'What changed?'* Like getting lost, knowing your starting point is key to arriving at your end point. So, infusing the whole learning environment with a reflective mindset is really beneficial.

2 *Every reflection is useful reflection.* I cover this more in **Activity 8**, but reflection is embedded and normalised by empowering everyone – teachers, Careers professionals, parents, assistants, other learners – in the learning environment whom learners engage with to ask good reflective questions.

3 *Confidence is sometimes a good proxy for learning.* We often start and end workshops by asking students how confident they feel on a scale of 1–10 or 1–5 about one of the elements we will be focusing on, such as making a Career decision, talking about their Skills, or speaking to an employer. You can ask that question again at the end, and then align that to a journey stage.

4 *Knowledge gain is sometimes a good proxy for learning.* This might seem more obvious: giving value to facts and information gained underpins what is sometimes an instinctive Careers journey. A learner might know 'in their gut' that they do or do not want to do something but cannot tell you why. So, focusing on what knowledge has been gained can open the door to reflection.

5 *Formal reflective learning gain is incredibly useful after a Careers interaction.* Giving learners ways to recognise their learning gain is extremely valuable and will help them see impact from your whole Careers programme, and not just their interactions with you.

6 *Remember your definition of success, and make that clear for learners, colleagues, and parents: learners who know where they are and which way they should be heading.* Yes, the Embark stage for all is a great aspiration, but self-aware learners are likely to make better decisions, whatever stage they are at. And not everyone who seems to start in Embark can credibly explain what they want to do and why.

Messages for learners

I know where I was when I started this activity; I know where I am now I've finished it

There are activities for me, whatever stage of my journey I am at

I know what will change for me as a result of doing/reading/engaging with this

I can tell you something I've learned from doing/reading/engaging with this

I can tell you how what I've learned has helped me understand something about myself

I can think about what I can do next.

Actions

- Try to start every Careers conversation with a learner by asking where they are on their Careers journey: are you Explore, Encounter, or Embark?
- Encourage everyone in the learning environment to become comfortable with self-identifying with the stages in the Careers journey and asking each other about it
- Develop some reflective questions for teachers, parents, and other learners to ask learners (see **Activity 8** also)
- Develop some 'confidence' questions
  - How confident do you feel about where to find information about ...?
  - How confident do you feel about explaining why X (alumni, parent, famous person) made their decision to start that business?
  - How confident do you feel about knowing what really interests you?
  - How confident do you feel about how to choose an apprenticeship/A level subject/university?
- Encourage the value of Careers knowledge gain alongside academic knowledge gain
  - What do you know now that you didn't know before?
  - And how does that help you know more about what you want/what interests you/what you want to do?'
- Develop a short formal reflective process for your key interactions, particularly one-to-one, group learning, and employer/FE/HE talks or visits
  - Ask before and after questions: What stage were you in before we started this? What stage are you in now?
  - Ask learners for something they now know about themselves that they didn't know before
  - Ask learners what they need to do next to move their journey along
- **Activity 9** also shows how to capture data from asking these questions that evidences the learning gain.

Context value

In taking this approach to embedding reflection, you are addressing the needs of each learner without resorting solely to personal guidance (Benchmark 3). Building a foundation where the learner owns their own learning, and doesn't solely rely on teachers and Careers professionals, enables them to develop increasingly a reflective mindset in all their Careers and other thinking. It also underpins a stable programme of Careers education because reflection is core to good learning (Benchmark 1).

Activity 7: Make work experience meaningful

Before we explore this Activity, I want to acknowledge three things. Firstly, this is a huge section of the book. The reason for that is that work experience has taken on significant value and emphasis in how Careers is discussed in school and college provision. In my opinion, this disproportionately ramps up the pressure on those who organise it, given how relatively little of it is sometimes available to learners.

I think that makes your lives as Careers Leaders, Careers professionals, and teachers more difficult than necessary, so, secondly, I want to acknowledge how incredibly challenging organising work experience can be. I have had to do it myself, and I have also been contacted many times about offering it. So, the ideas in this section are focused on how to maximise the benefit of what you are offering and/or your learners can access. But there are also some suggestions here about how to think about types of opportunities that may be useful and help you see work experience from a new point of view.

Thirdly, I want to acknowledge that the COVID pandemic has transformed the opportunities for employers and learners to engage with each other. Initially, it was indisputable that this was in a very negative way because normal activities were suspended. Even as we explore new ways of working and possible future normalities, employers, businesses, and organisations of all shapes and sizes are wondering what the future holds socially and economically, and how work might be transformed as we knew it pre-pandemic. That means that workplace-based experience for learners and students has been reshaped fundamentally.

These are therefore challenging times, but I believe we should not lose sight of the opportunity the pandemic has presented for looking differently at how employers and learners engage with each other, in order to preserve the value of life-wide learning beyond school and college. Because in the future, whatever our world looks like and whatever evolves and emerges, learners will get jobs because employers will need employees. So, this is an opportunity to think innovatively about how to get the value for your learners from interacting with an employer, but exploring how that might be achieved in a different way. I hope also that normalising virtual approaches might encourage more employers to engage with learners, because some of the traditional risks and obstacles that sometimes emerge or are perceived with workplace-based experiences are lessened by virtual interactions. I have therefore made some suggestions at the end of this section about how to create virtual work experience opportunities that are meaningful (with a bit more detail on different activities in Appendix 3).

We also need to recognise that for some learners (and through no fault of their school or college), work experience opportunities are incredibly rare, and we are all aware of the disparity of opportunity and its impacts. Formulas seem to have emerged around what work experience should look like at school and college level, and there appears to be an artificial distinction emerging around what is useful experience and what is not. It is also unfortunately the area where the learner's social capital often has greatest influence, and where those learners without social capital seem to be most disadvantaged.

This is one of the reasons that interactions with employers and workplaces are in the statutory guidance and the Benchmarks, but making it obligatory does not address learners' ability to gain benefit from it. I think a greater issue is, as I have outlined earlier in this book, that without a framework of learning gain where the learner can understand what difference an experience makes to them, they can have all the opportunities in the world but still make no progress on their Careers journeys. Or, if an experience finally becomes available, a learner does not know how they can make the most of it. So, every learner needs to be able to say, 'I know what has changed for me.'

To help you achieve that, in this Activity I explore the fundamental elements of work experience, discuss how to realise the meaningfulness of work experience using the Careers learning journey, and demonstrate how to develop virtual work experience delivery.

Fundamental elements

If something changes for the learner every time they interact with a workplace, how can we make clear to them what that change is, before they even speak to an employer or set foot in a workplace?

Whether we think of 'experiences of work' such as using a leisure facility, buying clothes, watching a sport training session, or 'work experiences' such as visiting a factory, shadowing a marketing manager, reading data on a screen, or actual employment in a retail store, *all* encounters and interactions with a workplace have two fundamental elements in common when it comes to learning gain for the learner. But we do not always make those clear.

Firstly, *every interaction builds an understanding of work-readiness.* A learner's fundamental understanding of work-readiness will always be enhanced when they:

- Are introduced to work, roles, and sectors by an employer or other professional
- Observe people working

- Understand workplace expectations
- Develop insight and understanding of the Knowledge, Attributes, Skills, and Experience required for effectiveness in the workplace.

As that happens, learners develop confidence and learn what they need to do to become work-ready. That is key to an effective transition to work, but also helps with decision-making.

Secondly, *every interaction creates an opportunity for reflection on Career choices*. In all interactions with a workplace, a learner is constantly evaluating and deciding whether they want to do a job like this or not, whatever the nature of their interaction with the work is. They might not be doing it very consciously, but at some instinctive level that evaluation is taking place. Surfacing that evaluation helps learners recognise that all these interactions support their Careers decision-making all the time. The learning gain is that every interaction is useful when recognised consciously.

As will become clear in the next section, these two learning gains are common to all work experiences, but as with all the previous Activities, and as we will see later when we explore Employability, we should not assume that learners are aware of this. So, you can achieve a great deal just by surfacing these two learning gains when you talk to learners about work.

The other key point worth recognising here is who 'owns' these two learning gains. As a Careers Leader, Careers professional, or teacher, you are a custodian of the learner's learning space, but it is important to recognise that the understanding of work-readiness is largely based on the employer's input to the experience, because they bring the context in which learners experience these elements. While you create all the reflective space for the learners, you do not generate all the content that is reflected upon, particularly when it comes to work-readiness. That will become useful to consider later, when we explore creating virtual work experiences.

Realising meaningfulness: Work experience in the Careers journey

As the earlier Activities have shown, if learners know where they are on their Careers journey – Explore, Encounter, or Embark – they will be able to identify what changes for them after an interaction. Just as with all other Careers interactions, the same experience will offer vastly different learning to different learners depending on what stage of their journey they are at.

I have identified four categories of benefit that learners gain from work experience, depending on where they are on their journey. As the detail in the coming pages shows, sometimes these are the same experiences which will have very different benefits, so this is not an introduction to four completely different categories of work experience. Many of the types of experiences I suggest below are experiences you are already offering or are available to your learners. But what is different is how we understand the benefit to your learners, and what learning they gain from those experiences depending on their Careers journey stage.

The four categories of benefit are as follows:

- Confidence-Building
- Careers Exploration
- Map-Making
- Entry Points.

Figure 14 shows how these categories align with the stages of the Careers journey.

Figure 14. Explore Encounter Embark: Categories of benefit for meaningful work experience

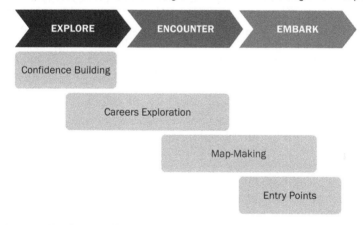

Illustration by Kalina Zlatkova. © Kate Daubney 2021.

While you will see many of the same types of experience listed in each of the categories, it is the lens through which the learner sees and reflects on that experience that makes the difference. So, there is much, much more that learners will gain from seeing all workplaces through those different lenses, than when you focus only on specific opportunities for different age groups.

Confidence-Building – EXPLORE

These interactions with the workplace are for learning about work for the first time, which begin to build confidence in the learner of their ability to make a Careers decisions based on a sound understanding of work. We traditionally think of first work experiences as being important for early exposure to Careers decision-making. But in my experience that initial exploration of their future selves is far more difficult for learners if they have not begun a process of really understanding what they want their experience of work to be. So, in this context, Explore does not just mean 'exploring my future Careers choices'. It also means 'exploring my future work behaviours and workplaces'.

We have all had conversations with learners where we find ourselves trying to manage their expectations while their imaginations roam freely across all possible future lives. We have all had to hold ourselves back from saying, 'You might not be as well suited to that as you think'. But these first work experiences and workplace interactions are not for proving us right or wrong. They are to enable learners to understand for themselves some of the fundamentals that underpin making decisions well, which are not about ability or aptitude or passion or interests. They are about understanding: 'This is what work is like. This is what workplaces are like. How confident can I be that this is what I want and is right for me?'

This reinforces our insight from our own working lives as well as in our capacity as Careers professionals that it is much harder to imagine yourself doing a particular job or choosing a Career path if you have not yet fully understood what it means to be and operate in the workplace, what the day-to-day rhythms and environment might be like, and whether you will like them. If you are easily bored by repetitive work, for example, laboratory testing processes or data analysis could completely undermine a love of science or an interest in numbers and patterns. Therefore, these opportunities give learners the chance to explore and set their own expectations of work, and not just dive into any number of possible future Careers.

In practice, most learners have informal interactions with the workplace all the time through parents, carers, and teachers, as well as through visiting retail spaces, leisure venues, food outlets, and so on. They may not think of those interactions as having anything to do with building confidence or understanding work-readiness, but that is where **Activities 6** and **8** become important, because learning to learn from everything needs in itself to be learned, enabled, and encouraged.

That is reinforced when we recognise how diverse the workplace experiences of our learners might already be. You will probably be aware from your school or college that those going into the workplace for the first time will include learners at two very different extremes:

- Learners who start working to earn money, such as in retail or food outlets or as apprentices, and so behaving as a paid employee, but …
  - They may otherwise never have had any workplace interactions at all
  - They may not see these as remotely relevant to their future Careers options
  - They may not have reflected on or learned from what it was like to work for the first time and become work-ready.

and

- Learners who are exploring Careers and work through shadowing, such as in one- or two-day visits, but …

o Do not have any responsibilities in that context
o See shadowing as about choosing a future Career path but do not see it as insight into how to function day-to-day in a role.

It would be easy to minimise what can be learned about Career decisions from either working in a fast food restaurant or sitting beside someone at a desk for two days. But both are immensely rich in value in terms of understanding work-readiness and what learners might or might not want their future working lives to be like. They are fundamental to building confidence in the learner of their ability to make decisions well about work, and not just to identify possible Careers choices. That is why these experiences are called Confidence-Building. They build the learner's confidence in themselves that they are gathering insights that enable future decisions to be made well.

Towards the end of this book, I focus specifically on the transition from education to work, but building self-confidence in advance of that transition and laying a foundation understanding of what it is to be ready to work should and can begin sooner than when education ends. Work experiences and interactions have a key part to play in laying that groundwork.

So, to summarise:

Confidence-Building opportunities offer:

- Learning about the workplace for the first time
- Observation of people working
  - Routines, tasks, behaviours, social interactions, use of technology, organisational structures
- Learning about workplace expectations of employees
- Learning about myself
  - What do I like and dislike?
  - Could I see myself in these roles, doing these tasks?
- Insight into what Knowledge, Attributes, Skills, and Experiences are required for effective workplace activities.

Types of Confidence-Building opportunities:

- Short workplace visits or video observations – one or two hours as a group in a structured visit, with talks and the opportunity to observe staff in action
- Work-shadowing for one day in person or online for an individual with a specific employer who understands the role of these experiences in building confidence and is well briefed
- Work-based activities brought into school or college with the opportunity to try tasks, look at equipment, or solve problems
- Problem-based or task-based learning in curriculum or co-curriculum, with clear Careers and Employability[1] connections articulated.

Learners will recognise and realise the benefits when you are also able to:

- Articulate what to look out for to learners, before a workplace visit or interaction
- Enable learners to reflect on what they learned about the workplace during and after the visit or interaction
  - 'That was busier/quieter than I expected', or 'It seems complicated/easier to get a task done than I expected'
- Enable learners to reflect on what they learned about themselves during and after the visit or interaction
  - 'I hate this' or 'That looks boring to me!'
- Brief employers in advance about the role of these experiences in building confidence about understanding workplaces and work behaviours
- Have discussions about what it means to be work-ready
  - For example, how might the way technology is used be different to school or my social life?
  - What does it sound like when people talk to each other about work activities? How is that different to me talking to a teacher or my friends?
- Hear alumni or employers talking about their first transition into work.

Careers Exploration – EXPLORE, ENCOUNTER

These interactions with the workplace are for exploring interests and preferences, challenging perceptions, shaping understanding, and laying the foundations for the first step into work. These interactions will have significant long-term impact if they are experienced with structured reflection built around them. As with Confidence-Building, learners will already have instinctive ideas about what looks interesting, fun, and rewarding through their existing informal interactions with workplaces, but reflection is needed around them to bring meaning to how learners begin to make Careers decisions. I remember being told when I was a teenager that work was 90 per cent boring. That shaped my expectations for a really long time and it wasn't until I was an adult and had been in work for some years that I realised I could define success for myself. I not only realised that it might not be true that work was 90 per cent boring, but if I was happy being 90 per cent bored, then that was also my choice.

These interactions also help to shape learners' priorities: what do they define as success in work terms? It is natural for learners thinking about Careers choices for the first time to focus on money, independence, and excitement: work will appear to offer a very stark contrast to the structures of education. But that also means that when it does not offer those benefits in the expected way, learners might quickly lose interest. As in the previous section, a platform of understanding work-readiness and having some confidence in what matters to them makes these easier to explore. So, putting other reference points in place for learners, such as what Skills they want to use or what sort of workplace they want to work in, helps them fill out in everyday practical ways the aspects we talk about in quite abstract, hypothetical ways in Careers guidance settings.

Again, these workplace interactions can take many forms, and while one week's experience can be a really significant platform for a learner to find their way with something they really enjoy, it can be a disaster for a learner who discovers on day one that they really hate it. I know that from my own teenage work experience week! Furthermore, if they do not get support in addressing why they hated it, the opportunity to gain value is lost, and confidence in the ability to use these explorations to make Careers decisions well can be quickly and easily undermined. It is really important, therefore, to frame work experiences of any length with the message that all experience is useful experience both for building confidence and making decisions, even if it does not turn out to be a 'good' experience.

To a large extent, this is the difference between an experience for an Explore learner and an Encounter learner. Ideally, an Explore learner is not going to go into a one-week experience with so much uncertainty attached that they risk having a difficult time because it does not meet their expectations. Conversely, an Encounter learner can benefit hugely from a whole week really digging down into the detail of something they think might be an option for them, and testing out their instincts. So, I think it is essential to make a distinction between Careers decision-making opportunities that are relevant to Explore and those relevant to Encounter, and I suggest that they should be of different types and lengths.

So, for *Explore* learners:

Careers Exploration experiences are about dipping into many different things, getting their bearings, imagining themselves in different situations, and developing their instincts. They are for gathering a range of relatively superficial snapshots that can start to reveal common themes that connect with discussions about interests and values.

Careers Exploration opportunities for Explore learners offer:

- The opportunity for an instinctive response
  - How do I feel about this?
- Observation of the appeal of what people do when they are working in different roles
  - Do I want to work in this way?
  - Do I want to work in an environment like this?
- Learning about workplace expectations of employees
  - Am I happy to meet those expectations?
- Learning about myself
  - What do I like and dislike?

- ○ Could I see myself in these roles, doing these tasks – and why, or why not?
- Insight into what Knowledge, Attributes, Skills, and Experiences are required for effective workplace activities, to connect with what they already can or cannot yet do
  - ○ This job involves meeting and talking to lots of people – I'd like to do that.

Types of Careers Exploration opportunities for Explore learners:

- Short workplace visits or video observations – one or two hours, preferably where the learner has chosen it out of interest or curiosity
- Work-shadowing for one day in person or online for an individual with a specific employer who understands the role of these experiences in exploration and is well briefed
- Work-based activities brought into school or college with the opportunity to try tasks, look at equipment, solve problems
- Problem-based or task-based learning in curriculum or co-curriculum, with clear Careers and Employability connections articulated
- Conversations with alumni one-to-one or in small groups where a detailed conversation can happen and sample activities explored informally.

And for *Encounter* learners:

Careers Exploration experiences are about less breadth and more depth. They are about building on initial instincts by reviewing and reflecting and trying things out more than once in different ways. They are about getting more than one insight into the same Career or study choice, or from a range of related perspectives (see also Map-Making below). They are for asking questions and responding to information gained, and testing out interests and values in different ways, and thinking about how the answers connect to what matters to the learner. This creates the shift from observing to analysing and reflecting.

Careers decision-making opportunities for Encounter learners offer:

- Longer or more than one opportunity to ask and reflect
  - ○ How do I feel about this?
  - ○ Why is this enjoyable/interesting?
- Analysis of what people do when they are working in different roles
  - ○ Why do I want to work in this way?
  - ○ Why do I want to work in an environment like this?
- Learning about workplace expectations of employees
  - ○ What would it mean if I were asked to meet those expectations?
  - ○ What would that mean I have to do?

- Learning about myself
    - What patterns or themes are emerging about Careers that interest me and Careers that don't?
    - If I choose very different things I'm interested in, do they have something in common or not?
    - And if not, what can I learn from that?
- Opportunities to identify specific Knowledge, Attributes, and Skills they want to develop or use in the workplace.

Types of Careers Exploration opportunities for Encounter learners:

- Longer workplace visits focusing on a specific role or activity, preferably where the learner has chosen it out of interest or curiosity
- Work-shadowing for two days either in person or online for an individual with a specific employee or group of employees in particular roles, who understand the role of these experiences in Careers decision-making and are well briefed
- Work-based activities brought into school or college with substantial projects attached for a half day or over a period of time
- Taster days with apprenticeship employers and training providers
- Problem-based or task-based learning in curriculum or co-curriculum, perhaps co-taught with an employer or role holder, with clear Careers and Employability connections articulated.

Whether in Explore or Encounter, learners will recognise and realise the benefits when you are also able to:

- Articulate what to look out for to learners, before a workplace visit or interaction
- Enable learners to reflect on what they learned about the workplace during and after the visit or interaction
    - 'That was busier/quieter than I expected' or 'It seems complicated/ easier to get a task done than I expected'
- Enable learners to reflect on what they learned about themselves during and after the visit or interaction
    - 'I hate this' or 'That looks boring to me!'
- Brief employers in advance about the role of these experiences in building confidence about understanding workplaces and work behaviours
- Have discussions about what it means to make decisions well, as opposed to making a 'right' decision
- Hear alumni or employers talking about how they explored their Careers choices for the first time.

Map-Making – ENCOUNTER, EMBARK

These interactions with the workplace are more for learners who are thinking of apprenticeships or school leaver programmes than further or higher education, in that they show a commitment to work as a choice and to the final stages of selecting a sector or role.[2] I call it Map-Making because it is all about getting to know the landscape of and around a likely Careers choice. It is like being a tourist in another country: without a map and a guidebook, it can be hard to maximise the benefit of the visit and make sure you see everything you want to see.

But it is also about the learner making the transition out of a mindset that says 'Choices are forced upon me!' and instead understanding and acting on the basis that 'I can choose what I want to do'. It is about not only mapping what is available but also choosing what matters on your map: on holiday, knowing where all the ice cream shops are might be more important than the medieval churches for some, but not for others. Making and taking ownership of those decisions are part of this transition through Encounter towards Embark, and about realising benefit from these sorts of experiences.

Experiences that fall under Map-Making are likely not to lead directly to employment (see Entry Points) but will give a lot of related, relevant insight into sectors and Career paths that will support the learner to make well-informed decisions and show valuable contextual knowledge to employers.

Map-Making opportunities have an important role to play in dispelling some of those inevitable nerves that learners have about feeling that if they choose not to continue in study, they are instead committing to 'One Career Forever!' through their first job. There is still so much distinction and separation drawn between education and work that some of that **Paralysis** I describe in the **Challenges** section is inevitable. It feels to learners like there is no going back after this point. In that context, it is no wonder that so many learners choose university instead of work because they perceive higher education as giving them a way to delay that inevitability.

But there is always a chance to 'go back'. Careers can be fluid, flexible, and meandering at all ages. The increasing emphasis on life-wide learning and the need to empower and enable people to respond to the sorts of economic and technological changes we are experiencing now mean that this distinction between education and work does not hold up to scrutiny. So, reflection that helps learners evaluate benefits and challenges, compare different experiences, and reflect on expectations and medium-term aspirations is critical to helping them develop confidence not only in their next choice, but in how to choose well.

That means that enabling learners to disentangle 'This is what all work will be like' from 'This is what *this* work will be like' is an important part of this process, which is why these experiences help bust myths, narrow options, challenge perceptions, and refine final choices. As with every other type of work experience opportunity, reflection is an essential component to help learners have confidence in these experiences and draw out their learning. Just like choices of qualifications, even into university where choice creates tension of a different sort, structured reflection helps learners understand that they are not making a final choice, but instead are simply choosing their next step at this time.

Map-Making opportunities for school and college learners can also help refine expectations and understanding of what work/study combinations will be like in structured programmes post-secondary and further education. They help learners define their priorities: work/study programmes are more highly structured than many choices in further or university education, which can feel incredibly unstructured after 11–18 education. But a learner who knows that they enjoy 'learning by doing' and has some reflective activity that helps them recognise that value through Map-Making experiences, will be able to embrace the fact that this approach to learning is more suited to their strengths.

In the wider sense, therefore, Map-Making experiences are not merely about figuring out 'What will this be like for me?' but also 'What will I bring to this?' In conjunction with enabling learners to understand their own Employability, learners can start to see themselves in work and the workplace. These types of work experiences help students refine their sense of what they offer in terms of the relevant Skills and Attributes, as well as specialist interest and perhaps Knowledge, for a particular role or sector. At school and college level, learners have not had the opportunity to accumulate most of those assets, but they will be more successful more quickly in their final choice of work/study programme if they have more self-awareness to be confident of why they are well suited to their choice.

As ever, these workplace interactions can take many forms, but at this stage of decision-making they would need to be reasonably detailed and specific experiences, if not long ones. Learners considering an apprenticeship, say, in building trades, digital, health and science, or hospitality, need to have the opportunity to explore their options across those sectors, and not just individual roles. So, schools and colleges can work with employers to discuss what would be a meaningful way for an employer to help a learner identify if they are suited to such an opportunity. This is more of a partnership in opportunity development.

It is also worth mentioning that one of the purposes these experiences serve at higher education level is to offer students a chance to get to know a sector where there are no established recruitment routes for graduates with development programmes, such as across the arts and heritage sectors, many parts of the media, charities, international development, or politics. These sectors are relatively much smaller than the corporate and industrial sectors, and at pre-18 level tend not to have entered strongly into apprenticeship routes either. These sectors may correlate more strongly with passions and interests learners have, and this is where the making of the map of such sectors becomes really valuable to learners. A learner who has volunteered in a heritage property or community arts project, for example, can get to know the roles, the financial flow through an organisation, and the training or qualifications established employees have, as well as exploring and refining their own interests and experiences. This also gives them access to networks of knowledge and opportunity that help underpin their decision-making and future experiences in landscapes that are often incredibly challenging to enter at any stage of working life.

To summarise, I would make a distinction between Map-Making opportunities that are relevant to the Encounter phase and those relevant to Embark, and suggest that they should be of different types and lengths.

For learners in *Encounter*:

These experiences are again about less breadth and more depth. As much as possible, in Map-Making experiences it is about reviewing and reflecting and trying things out more than once, in different ways if possible. It is about asking questions, testing out interests, and thinking about how the answers connect to what matters to the learner. As with Careers Exploration, it is the shift from observing to analysing and reflecting.

Map-Making opportunities for Encounter learners offer:

- The opportunity for a more considered response
  - How do I feel about this, now I'm getting to know more about it?
- Observation of the appeal of what people do when they are working in different roles
  - This is what *this* work will be like. How close is this to what I think I want?
- Learning about workplace expectations of employees
  - Am I happy to meet those expectations?
  - How will I feel when I am expected to work in this way?
- Learning about myself
  - What do I like and dislike?
  - Could I see myself in these roles, doing these tasks – and why, or why not?
  - Do I feel excited and enthusiastic about this?
  - How does it connect to what matters to me?
- Insight into what Knowledge, Attributes, Skills, and Experiences are required for effective workplace activities, to connect with what they already can or cannot yet do
  - This job involves meeting and talking to lots of new people every day – I'd like to do that.
- A glimpse into a future Career in this sector
  - What paths do people take?
  - What might my options be if I started here?

Types of Map-Making opportunities for Encounter phase learners:

- Longer workplace visits or virtual projects focusing on a specific role or activity, where the learner has chosen it out of interest in order to refine final choices
- Work-shadowing in person or online for two or more days for an individual with a specific employee or group of employees in particular roles,

who understand the role of these experiences in preparing to enter work and are well briefed

- Work-based activities brought into school or college with substantial projects attached for a half day or over a period of time
- Taster days with apprenticeship employers and training providers
- Problem-based or task-based learning in curriculum or co-curriculum, perhaps co-taught with an employer or role holder, with clear Careers and Employability connections articulated.

Encounter learners will recognise and realise the benefits when you are also able to:

- Enable learners to understand how to take ownership of their choices and what is important to them
  - Encourage and enable learners before a workplace interaction to identify what they want to look out for and learn about
  - Enable learners to learn how to reflect on the experience while they are there and act accordingly
  - Enable learners to identify what steps they need to take to fill in any gaps in information they feel they have
  - Enable learners to reflect on what they learned about themselves and their Career interests, and what steps they now need to take to fill in any gaps in self-awareness
- Brief employers in advance about the role of these experiences in preparing to enter work and make future Careers decisions well
- Continue discussions with learners about what it means to make decisions well, as opposed to making a 'right' decision
- Enable learners to discuss with alumni and employers how they evaluated their choices of Career.

For learners in *Embark*:

These experiences are about finalising the range of choices from which the next step will be chosen. It is a way of mapping a sector, particularly one that might be unfamiliar, so that the learner understands how choices fit together and connect to each other, including what next steps are available after this step. It is about gathering information to formulate a plan of how to move forward, where the learner moves from 'This is happening to me' to 'I know what my choices are and how to make my own decision'.

Map-Making opportunities for Embark phase learners offer:

- The opportunity for a considered, reflective response
  - What do I now know that helps me narrow down my final decision?
- Observation of the appeal of what people do when they are working in different roles
  - This is what *this* work will be like

- o What will learning to do this be like for me?
- Learning about workplace expectations of employees
  - o What will I need to do to meet those expectations?
- Learning about myself
  - o This is where I can see I will enjoy myself and pick up new Skills quickly
  - o This is where I might find some challenges, so I need to get advice on how to manage that
- Insight into what Knowledge, Attributes, Skills, and Experiences are required for effective workplace activities, to connect with what they already can or cannot yet do
  - o I can see why I am well suited to doing a role like this, and I can see where I'm going to be learning new Knowledge, and developing new Attributes and Skills
- A glimpse into a future Career in this sector
  - o What paths do people take?
  - o What might my options be if I started here?
  - o How could I see myself progressing if I started here?

Types of Map-Making opportunities for Embark phase learners:

- Longer workplace visits focusing on a specific role or activity, where the learner has chosen it out of interest in order to refine final choices
- Work-shadowing for up to a week for an individual in person or virtually, hopefully including a short project or specific tasks, hosted by a specific employee or group of employees in particular roles who understand the role of these experiences in preparing to enter work and are well briefed
- Work-based activities brought into school or college with substantial projects attached over significant periods of time
- Taster days with employers or training providers, where the learner has already begun to narrow their choices, and can attend with specific questions
- Problem-based or task-based learning in curriculum or co-curriculum, perhaps co-taught with an employer or role holder, with clear Careers and Employability connections articulated.

Embark learners will recognise and realise the benefits when you are also able to:

- Enable learners to take ownership of their choices and what is important to them
  - o Learners deciding for themselves what they need to look for and reflect on, before they start the experience

- o Enabling learners to reflect continuously on what they are learning about the sector, role, and workplace, and what steps they need to take to finalise any missing information relevant to a decision
  - o Enabling learners to reflect continuously on what they are learning about themselves and their Career interests, and what steps they now need to take to fill in any gaps in self-awareness
- Brief employers in advance about the role of these experiences in finalising next Careers decisions
- Have discussions about what it means to make decisions well
- Have discussions about what future decisions might arise and enable learners to feel confident that they know how to make them
- Enable learners to discuss with alumni and employers how they finalised their first Careers choice and how they look at ongoing professional development decisions.

Entry Points – EMBARK

These interactions with the workplace are the final gateway to apprenticeships or school leaver programmes, in that they show a commitment to a specific role or sector as a choice.[3] At higher education level, I would describe these experiences as 'causal', in that a summer internship with an employer might lead directly to an offer of future employment. A learner commits to this type of work experience to finalise their Career decision about their next step, and begin to get the relevant experience to make a smooth transition and a successful start.

These opportunities are not as well established in a structural sense at school and college level, when compared to higher education, although increasingly employers and training providers are creating taster days and other short programmes to give learners easier ways to engage with their future options. But given that the Institute for Apprenticeships and Technical Education describes would-be apprentices in its definition of a Quality Apprenticeship as being 'motivated to learn and work diligently to complete their apprenticeship',[4] it is increasingly important that learners are given ways to establish that motivation, through sufficient access to information and experiences to build confidence in their decisions.

If relevant taster days do not exist, more effort might be required by the learner, with support from the school or college, to create a relationship with a future employer or training provider to find out more. I think it is important here that the school or college does not own this process for the learner (not least because you do not have the capacity to do so!) but actively supports the learner to own it themselves, for example by giving feedback on an introductory email the learner has written to an employer, or sitting in while a learner makes a phone call to an employer. If a large number of your learners are entering this route, you may already have developed some content around writing introductory emails or suggested scripts for making first phone calls to help with this. One of the key areas we see students in higher education struggle with is the transition to taking responsibility for their own opportunities. So it is really valuable to enable learners to become agents and owners of their own outcomes as early and as quickly as possible.

Learners having Entry Point experiences are still very likely to have some of those nerves about committing to 'One Career Forever!' through their first job. In a sense, it is inevitable that they return to the simple realisation of 'This is what work will be like!' But a learner who has made a well-informed, self-aware decision can be reassured and reassure themselves that this choice has not come out of the blue. Again, it is important to remind learners that this is just the next step, but also that good Map-Making means that they know what their next steps after this can be across both work and further study. As I noted earlier, there is no such thing as a bad decision; it might just take the learner longer to get to their destination if they take a route that they later decide was not quite right for them, or they want to try something different.

Hopefully by this stage, reflection and self-awareness are becoming pretty well embedded, but giving learners regular check-ins with Careers Leaders, Careers professionals, and teachers, as well as with other learners who are choosing a similar path, is really helpful.

Entry Point opportunities for Embark learners offer:

- The opportunity for a considered, reflective response
  - What do I now know about my next step that helps me make a smooth transition into it?
- Observation of the appeal of what people do when they are working in different roles
  - This is what *this* work will be like
  - How can I get ready to start working like this?
- Learning about workplace expectations of employees
  - What do I still need to do to prepare myself to meet those expectations?
  - How might I keep myself motivated if it is harder than I think, to begin with?
- Learning about myself
  - This is where I can see I will enjoy myself and pick up new Skills quickly
  - This is where I might find some challenges, so I can use this opportunity to find out where to get advice on how to manage that once the job starts
- Insight into what Knowledge, Attributes, Skills, and Experiences are required for effective workplace activities, to connect with what they already can or cannot yet do
  - I can see why I am well suited to doing a role like this, and I can see where I'm going to be learning new Knowledge, and developing new Attributes and Skills.

Types of Entry Point opportunities for Embark learners:

- Work-shadowing for at least a week or longer for an individual, out of term time, hopefully including a short project or specific tasks either in person or virtually, hosted by a specific employee or group of employees in particular roles who understand the role of these experiences in preparing to enter work and are well briefed
- Work-based activities brought into school or college with substantial projects attached over significant periods of time
- Problem-based or task-based learning in curriculum or co-curriculum, perhaps co-taught with an employer or role holder, with clear Careers and Employability connections articulated.

Embark learners will recognise and realise the benefits when you are also able to:

- Enable learners to take ownership of their choices and what is important to them
  - Learners decide for themselves what they need to look for and reflect on, before they start the experience
  - Learners know how to reflect continuously on what they are learning to enable their successful transition into the job, but also to make a strong start
  - Learners know how to reflect continuously on what they are learning about themselves and their Career interests, to help them realise when they are succeeding in the job and manage challenges if they arise
- Brief employers in advance about the role of these experiences in preparing to enter work
- Enable learners to connect with alumni in similar roles or sectors, for ongoing conversations and reflection opportunities.

Creating virtual work experiences

As I mentioned in the introduction to this section, the pandemic has forced us to think differently about many aspects of in-person experiences. But as many Careers Leaders, Careers professionals, and teachers know, organising workplace visits or work experiences can already be fraught with all sorts of logistical issues that sometimes feel prohibitively difficult to overcome, from health and safety assessments to risk assessments to the sheer organisational logistics of getting a large number of learners into a workplace, or getting employers on board and well briefed. So, exploring how we can achieve much of the same learning through virtual means makes a lot of sense in any context, and that becomes particularly important if in-person opportunities dry up.

But what is it that employers actually offer when they invite learners in? It can feel very mysterious and largely invisible and, when we are stretched for time and mental energy, quite overwhelming to unravel. I recognise it might be equally overwhelming to read here that you might be able to create a form of virtual work experience for your school or college, or even partner with a new employer who wants to help out by offering something virtual but does not know how!

In this section, therefore, I return to those very basic elements of what work experiences offer that I outlined at the start of **Activity 7**. These apply whether for virtual or in-person experiences, whatever journey stage your learners are at. I draw those together with some of the resources you are probably already using as informational learning. This creates the backbone of a virtual work experience programme you can create yourself, and a template you can share with an employer who wants to offer something virtual but may not know how. There are also some suggestions for new content you might create with employers and teaching colleagues for your learners if you have capacity.

What are the basic elements of work experience?

I outlined at the start of **Activity 7** the importance to learners of understanding work-readiness, and I indicated that it is employers who own this information. We have a role as Careers Leaders, Careers professionals, and teachers to create appropriate spaces and ways to reflect on that, but employers define what they are looking for in work-readiness.

So, whatever Careers journey stage your learners are at, their fundamental understanding of work-readiness will always be enhanced when they:

- Are introduced to work, roles, and sectors by an employer or other professional
- Observe people working
- Understand workplace expectations
- Develop insight and understanding of the Knowledge, Attributes, Skills, and Experience required for effectiveness in the workplace.

And when we think about how employers shape that learning, it divides into three key themes:

- Introducing the workplace context
  - What does the workplace physically look like?
  - What is a working day like?
  - What relationships exist to create the workplace and get the work done?
- Employer voice
  - What is it like to do this role?
  - How did I make the decision to do this role or follow this Career path?
  - How did I get into this role and sector?

- o What Knowledge, Attributes, Skills, and Experience did I already have and what have I had to learn and develop in the role?
- o What does a day look like, both typically and atypically?
- Tasks and simulations
  - o What are the common tasks of this role?
  - o What problems do I solve?
  - o What decisions do I make?
  - o Who do I work with, and why are those interactions important to the role?
  - o What Knowledge, Attributes, Skills, and Experiences are required to complete tasks?

But how do we make these fit together? When we are working with employers, their opportunities are framed around their expectations of future employees, but they may be unaware of the needs or profiles of the learners they might be meeting, and/or may not fully understand what Careers education and Employability development seek to achieve from the learner's point of view. Thus to manage expectations for everyone – employer, learner, school/college – it helps to map how the learners' understanding of work-readiness can be created by the different elements of employer input.

Figure 15 shows how this mapping might look. This is useful when you are considering what an in-person work experience offers, but when we start thinking about how we might create a virtual experience, it also gives us a set of clear reference points for what we want the learning gain for learners to be. Whatever the means through which a virtual experience is delivered, whether through a virtual learning environment or a series of live interactions using an online meeting platform, it should not and need not be distinctly different from our expectations for an in-person experience. There may be specific hurdles or factors that the virtual and digital element creates, but the core learning gain has to be the same.

When you review the table in Figure 15 you will hopefully already have some of the content in your current resources and information for learners. (Anything in the table marked with an asterisk is covered in more detail in Appendix 3 at the end of the book.) And when you meet new employers, or you want to revisit your partnerships with existing employers, alumni, and parents, there are activities in Figure 15 and Appendix 3 that you can ask them to create for you and with you, particularly videos, podcasts, problems, scenarios, simulations, and other pre-prepared materials that will build up your library of resources.

How do I build a virtual work experience?

When you build a virtual work experience, you are not necessarily aiming to do all of these activities mapped in the table. What you are aiming to do is to ensure that each of the key areas the learner needs (listed in the left-hand column – introduction, observation, understanding, and insight) are met in at least one way by the employer's interaction with learners. If possible, you

Figure 15. Mapping learners' needs for virtual work experiences

LEARNERS NEED...	INTRODUCING THE WORKPLACE CONTEXT	EMPLOYER VOICE	TASKS AND SIMULATIONS	INDIVIDUAL AND PEER/GROUP REFLECTION
Introductions to work by an employer/professional	Online learning: videos, reading, podcasts	Live virtual Q&A with an employer or professional Virtual panel events	Problem-based learning*	Logbooks and journals First impressions: what interests me and what doesn't?
Observations of people working	Online learning: videos	Day in the Life videos*		Logbooks and journals First impressions: describing and reflecting on tasks and activities, patterns of work and workplaces
Understanding of workplace expectations	Situational judgement exercises* Online learning about Professionalism*	Live virtual Q&A with an employer or professional Virtual panel events	Business games Design simulations	Logbooks and journals
Developing insight and understanding of the knowledge, attributes, skills and experience required for effectiveness in the workplace	Online learning: videos, reading, podcasts - focusing on the needs for specialist knowledge, specialist skills, attributes and transferable skills	Learners interview employers*	Role-specific/Skill-specific tasks and simulations* Problem-based learning* Business games Design simulations	Logbooks and journals Learners interview employers* Roleplay* Situational judgement exercises*

Table design by Kalina Zlatkova. © Kate Daubney 2021.

should also try to include some reflection activity (the last column in the table) to help make sense of the experience with and for your learners.

So, for example, you might create a virtual experience that looks like this. The activities in italics are reflective opportunities that can scaffold the employer interactions and use of resources.

- *Preparation: Explore, Encounter, Embark: Which stage am I at?*
    - *What do I want to be different after I have this experience?*
    - *What kind of learning gain do I want?*
        - *Confidence-Building, Careers Exploration, Map-Making*

- Introduction to work, roles, and sectors by an employer or other professional
    - Live Employer Q&A
    - *Post-interaction journal or logbook entry, or Peer Discussion*

- Observation of people working
    - Day in the life video
    - *Group or Peer discussion*

- Understanding workplace expectations
    - Situational judgement exercise
    - *Group discussion of exercise answers*

- Develop insight and understanding of the Knowledge, Attributes, Skills, and Experience required for effectiveness in the workplace
    - Problem-based learning
    - Role-specific simulation
    - *Employer feedback and Group discussion.*

I have indicated that this model might work for the first three categories of work experience, but not for Entry Points: in that case, you would want the employer to be offering more specific activities that are related to the role the learners are moving into.

What you can see from this model is that a virtual experience is not about completely replicating an in-person experience through digital means. Digital education offers a diverse range of approaches and learning styles in itself and at the time of writing its full potential is still being realised in traditional education, let alone in relation to work-based learning. Indeed, there is an entire body of scholarship dedicated to how to use digital education tools to diversify learners' engagement and learning experiences which is not harnessed specifically here. However, what the model does demonstrate is how we can capture the elements of the workplace interaction effectively and discretely, and explore diverse ways to deliver those through digital means, rather than trying to replicate an entire block of time in a workplace. Adopting a more granular or fragmented approach may enable you to engage more learners over a longer period of time using more diverse means.

You can also see from this model and from Figure 15 that the extent to which an employer might be directly involved in delivering this virtual experience is quite variable. But whatever structure or combination of activities you use, it remains essential to brief employers effectively before they get involved. Many employers, particularly smaller ones, are highly focused on keeping their businesses afloat in challenging times, but if they are eager to contribute, you can quickly get a lot of benefit from a conversation that makes it clear how their input supports your learners, and what the benefits to them will be. Employers are looking for self-aware learners with an interest in what is on offer, so if you can help employers to recognise how their contribution supports learners to achieve that, everyone benefits.

Activity 7: Summary

This activity has covered a great deal of content, which demonstrates the importance of putting interactions with work in context. From surfacing work-readiness and conscious awareness of decision-making, to using the Three Stage Careers Journey to help learners identify how an interaction moves them forward, there is a massive amount of additional value that you can realise from what you are already doing with learners to make work experiences more meaningful.

Creating virtual experiences does take time and organisation, and it will be interesting to see how employers develop their own ideas about how to offer something to school and college learners in this way as post-pandemic work reshapes. But the ideas above should help you think differently about what we mean when we talk about workplace interactions, and to initiate conversations of your own with employers about collaborating to create virtual content that should have considerable value and longevity.

Key principles and Actions for you

- Surface the fundamentals
  - Work-readiness and Careers decision-making are evolving through every interaction, whether experiences of work or work experiences
- Context is essential
  - Signpost to learners how different types of work experience fit with different stages of the Careers journey
- Create some learning gains so learners go into an experience with an idea of what to expect and how it will influence their Careers journey
  - Articulate to learners before a workplace interaction what to look out for
  - Enable learners to reflect on what they learned about the workplace
  - Enable learners to reflect on what they learned about themselves
- Be clear with learners that they share responsibility for realising the benefit of an experience

- o Whether it is towards work or further study, learners need to enter with the understanding that they are on a journey to take full ownership of what they ultimately choose to do next
- All experiences are useful for learning
  - o From 1 day work-shadowing to company-sponsored insight schemes, from working in a fast food outlet to following a high-ranking friend of the family, from situational judgement to task simulations, the only pointless experience is one that a learner doesn't learn from
- Articulate to employers what type of opportunity they are hosting or capturing and how they can support learners to benefit
  - o Direct liaison and briefings, or briefings for learners to share with employers, are really important for framing expectations and maximising benefit for all.

Messages for learners

I know where I was when I started this workplace interaction or experience; I know where I am now I've finished it

There are workplace interactions and experiences for me, whatever stage of my journey I am at

I know what will change for me as a result of engaging with this

I can tell you something I've learned from engaging with this

I can tell you how what I've learned has helped me to understand something about myself

I can think about what I can do next

There's no such thing as a bad decision; it might just take me longer to get to my destination if I take a route that I later decide wasn't quite right for me

When I enter work as my next Career step, I will take on more responsibility for my learning and how I benefit from what I do, learn, and think.

Context value

In taking the approaches above to making work experiences meaningful, you are addressing the needs of each pupil (Benchmark 3), maximising the benefit of all the encounters with employers, employees, and workplaces (Benchmarks 5 and 6 (and 7 if you are doing the same with higher education)), and providing a platform for personal guidance to be more effective (Benchmark 8). Likewise, connecting encounters with employers, employees, and workplaces into the Careers journey provides a more stable Careers programme (Benchmark 1).

Notes

1   The connection to Employability will make more sense when you read the second half of this book, but in essence this refers to the application of transferable Skills and Attributes that develop in different subjects, and not to a linear connection between a subject and a future job.

2   Many universities offer programmes of taster courses or summer schools to enable learners to try out different subjects, including those that are not on offer in schools and colleges.

3   University taster courses and summer schools are likewise incredibly helpful for managing learner expectations about the difference between being taught and learning independently.

4   https://www.instituteforapprenticeships.org/quality/what-is-a-quality-apprenticeship/ (accessed 8 April 2020).

Activity 8: Make conversations meaningful

I have alluded to this several times already in this book, but I believe it is important enough to make it a separate activity here. Every conversation a learner has with a Careers Leader, Careers professional, or teacher will actively contribute to their Careers journey. It is not about asking staff who have no experience (or interest) in Careers and Employability to suddenly cross their comfort zone or become experts in that too. But it is about everyone learning to ask open questions and enable reflective discussion with learners. There are some added key areas that might specifically point to the Careers or Employability value of a conversation between a learner and a teacher, but this is also about impactful everyday conversation.

In higher education, there often exists a perceived divide between the role of academics and that of Careers services, and sometimes that divide is made more complex or ambiguous when academic colleagues take on pastoral Tutor roles. As I outlined in **Challenge 5** about **Neuroscience**, learners are going through complex intellectual, emotional, and social change, and life is generally not tidy! Conversations that start out being about academic matters can morph into conversations about personal matters, and as I know from personal experience during my professional life as an academic, that can be disorientating.

The ecosystems of influence that exist around learners are increasingly complex: social media has the potential to connect all of us to people we do not know, apparently as intimately as to those we do. For learners who are looking for reference points to build their values, interests, and identity, those can be powerful forces that are not always immediately visible to us as Careers Leaders, Careers professionals, and teachers. There will also be diverse factors at play in learners' domestic lives which will shape a learner's view of their future, yet which may remain very hidden even in a one-to-one guidance setting.

So, it is important that we recognise that, even if we are not seeing obvious evidence of it, learners frequently perceive their teachers and Careers educators as a highly experienced source of wisdom outside their peer and family communities, when it comes to future lives. It is not my role as author of this book to ask anyone to do more or take on responsibilities that they are not comfortable with. But as you will have picked up by now, I do think it is useful for everyone to think about how they might realise more value for learners from what they already do, and this is no exception.

This matters for a number of reasons. I will outline below how meaningful con-versations can contribute to effective Careers decision-making, but the broader value centres again on the importance of self-awareness, which we know is highly valued by employers. For example, a learner who can identify who influ-ences them, and how and why, is likely to be more alert to how their interactions with employers and higher education shape their next decision. Likewise, a learner who gets used to digging a little deeper into their instinctive responses to curricu-lum activities develops a stronger analytical framework which will help them determine more easily what they enjoy and what interests them. Employers are embarking on potentially quite long journeys of self-development with new employees, whether at 16, 18, or after higher education: the more self-aware the learner is, the easier that journey is to begin and continue. Thus, every conversa-tion with a learner helps develop and shape their self-awareness.

In the school or college

I will elaborate on the curriculum-based aspects of meaningful conversations in much more detail in the Employability section of this book.[1] But developing meaningful conversations in relation to curriculum is important in all educa-tional contexts because it builds learners' ability to be reflective, and have confidence in getting to know themselves.

The traditionally didactic approach to teaching is evolving and changing as more schools introduce additional reflective structures and opportunities inside and outside curriculum, and increased virtual and online learning has only rein-forced that. But asking questions that not only focus on learning, but the value *to the learner* – and not just to the curriculum – of what has been learned can quickly enhance the sort of self-reflection that is useful on the Careers journey. Teaching in the Personal, Social, Health, and Economic (PSHE) curriculum will already provide a platform for some of this, and in some schools and colleges PSHE is used to align with Careers conversations too.

For example, in a subject-based curriculum setting, a 'Knowledge' question can spawn self-awareness questions helpful in Careers exploration:

- Can you tell me something new that you learned today?
  Introduces ...
    o What did that tell you about what interests you?
    o What did that tell you about what you find fun?
    o What did that tell you about what you find easy or hard?
    o Imagine a time when you might find that useful outside this class-room. *Or* How do you think that might be useful to someone who isn't in this classroom?
    o If you were trying to pinpoint where you are on the journey to learn more about this, are you near the beginning, the middle, or the end – at least for now?

Likewise, a 'Skills' question can also spawn self-awareness questions helpful in Careers exploration:

- What was the skill that you were using today?

  Introduces …
  - Does it remind you of any other Skills?
  - Do you find it easy or hard?
  - Do you feel a sense of accomplishment when you get something right using that skill?
  - Imagine a time when you might use that skill outside this classroom.
  - If you were trying to pinpoint where you are on the journey to learn more about this skill and how to use it, are you near the beginning, the middle, or the end – at least for now?

And ultimately, in any learning and non-learning setting, 'why' and 'how' questions are always really useful, such as:

- Why do you think that?
- How do you think that happens?
- Why does that matter to you?
- How might that change other things you know?
- Why is that useful to you?
- Why is that useful to someone else?
- How might you see that being different in the future?
- What could you learn that might change your mind about that and why?
- How could you see that from a completely different point of view?
- How could you make progress on thinking about this? What else might you need to find out?

This approach can be adopted by everyone in the learning environment. Encouraging and enabling teachers and other educators, as well as employers who are in school/college, to use open-ended and consciously reflective questions with learners during informal conversation go a long way towards building a platform of self-awareness that becomes really valuable in Careers and Employability terms.

Furthermore, empowering peer groups to have these discussions collectively is also incredibly useful. Depending on the ages of the learners, it may help to have a Careers Leader, Careers professional, or teacher in a moderating capacity – younger learners may need more structure to a conversation than older learners – and you may want to bring specific themes to a discussion so it has some sense of focus and progress to it. I mentioned earlier using discussions about alumni or famous people's journeys as a good platform for exploration and reflection. Peer-to-peer learning has been explored extensively in academic research, particularly as the internet and social media have become more significant in learners' lives, but it is still relatively under-used. It does require some ground rules around respect, confidentiality, and how to give positive critical feedback, but giving learners a safe space in small groups to explore their self-awareness together is really valuable.

Outside school or college

Supporting learners in their home environment is naturally more complicated, and is highly dependent on who the learner has around them by way of peers, family, carers, and other people. Introducing the 'why' and 'how' questions for learners themselves to use when they read or watch something is a good platform, but there will also be times where parents and other adults may become involved in some of the key decision-making about next stages.

Empowering learners to define for themselves what a useful discussion looks like for them is a really important part of this, and offsets both the **Hourglass Phenomenon (Challenge 1)** and the **Paralysis** issue (**Challenge 3**). The combination of our educational processes, social frameworks, and neuroscience means that learners often feel that decisions happen to them, particularly when adults give well-meaning advice. So, enabling learners to find ways to say things like, 'OK, but something my school wants me/I want to think about is *why* that matters to me' can be very valuable. Giving them short, accessible lists of reflective questions that sit around these decision-making points will reinforce these are normal questions to ask, and that will make it easier for them to draw on them.

If peer learning is working well in your learning environment, it can also be really useful outside it. Learners who are going on visits to workplaces or universities together can be encouraged to reflect together as well as independently. Also, learners may feel more comfortable having these conversations in more informal time; it is not only the educators' comfort zone which can feel challenged by these conversations and changes, but the learners' too. You may find that learners are using online platforms to exchange views; these do have a use, but can also be relatively unmonitored and so may include quite a bit of inaccurate information. You can challenge carefully if you hear a learner repeat something unsubstantiated, but also use it to help a learner identify why something they have read feels meaningful to them.

Briefing parents and carers is important, if you have the means to do so. I have met and worked with thousands of parents and carers during my career, at university open days, at conferences, in schools, and more recently as an employer myself. At a time of considerable instability and uncertainty, they are increasingly looking to institutions and organisations for stability and certainty, so this is a good time to be establishing more consistent approaches to briefing parents and carers, not only on the processes around key decisions but also on the context in which learners make those decisions in your school or college. In the **Actions** below, I give you some ideas about how to do that.

If you are able to establish a consistent approach across your school or college to how reflection is built in to daily life, then sharing that also with parents and carers as a normalised approach to how learners learn will reinforce the value of this happening outside school or college as well as inside. Parents and carers mostly will not have had this sort of support or thinking during their education and may have a range of responses from, 'This is nothing to do with me' to 'I know exactly what the right thing for X to do is, and it's not what the school is telling me it is.'

Engaging parents and carers to be part of the conversation is about helping them feel comfortable to take part and helping them see that they have a role and a contribution to make. But it is also giving them a different way to fulfil that role and make a contribution that is more about enabling the learner and less about validating the role of the parent or carer as a valuable reference point. It is not that they are not valuable, but when everything is in constant change and flux, that value is most often brought by being a reflective companion for the learner, and not necessarily by bringing their own perspective or experience or showing that they might know everything. That can be a difficult message for parents and carers to hear, so helping them see what alternative roles they can valuably fill is a proactive step worth taking.

There is also a key question about whether you should share with parents and carers the definition of success I outlined earlier: that we want learners to be self-aware, know where they are on their Careers journey, and which way they are heading. This can be a controversial viewpoint, particularly because it is unfamiliar, and because it is not measurable in the way that other things are (though **Activity 9** will show you how you can measure it!). So, it will seem relatively unimportant to parents and carers when compared with key process-related decisions being made and grades being achieved. You may, therefore, choose to keep it to yourself and position the importance of self-awareness through its value to employers. This will seem less controversial and more convincing. However, I would strongly encourage you to make this visible as *a* definition of success, if not *the* definition of success. Parents and carers – particularly those who have not been to university or may be unfamiliar with the range of opportunities on offer – may not realise the role they can play in supporting that self-awareness. With some light touch guidance and framing from you, they can adopt that role very impactfully.

If you have particularly effective engagement with your parent and carer community, you could also outline the **Challenges** and the **Environment** factors from the start of this book, to help parents and carers make sense of the landscape and obstacles learners face. This may also help lessen some of the pressure that parents and carers inadvertently place on learners. Likewise, if you are already running briefings and meetings on the key decision points such as choosing GCSEs, you may also want to build on those with more information about what the Three Stage Careers Journey looks like in that context. For example, an Encounter learner might be having trouble choosing between Music and another language, so what questions might a parent or carer be able to ask that helps the learner understand how to make that decision well, rather than to make the 'right' decision.

Employers

I discussed in **Activity 7** the importance of making clear the role that employers play in supporting effective decision-making by learners. They might well feel that they are doing a lot already by offering an opportunity, but giving them support in how to have meaningful and effective conversations with learners can often be more welcome than you might think.

Like parents and carers, employers can often feel slightly out of touch with how things are done unless they have children of their own or are connected in other ways to schools or colleges. They also have a lot to do, just doing their own jobs! Like teachers, parents, and carers, employers are likely to feel that they are outside their comfort zone in having conversations like these, particularly if they have not had experience themselves of any kind of organisational development that focused on their own Career journey. So, any pointers you give them about how to start and continue conversations that are meaningful to the learner may well be welcome. There are some ideas to try in the **Actions** section below.

Key principles for you

1 *Reflection is the best way to cement learning gain and answer the question, 'What changed?'* Empowering the learner and everyone around them to feel more confident exploring the learner's self-awareness is the foundation for better decision-making.

2 *Every reflection is useful reflection.* As in **Activity 6**, empowering everyone in the learning environment that learners engage with – teachers, Careers professionals, parents, employers, other learners – to ask good reflective questions constantly embeds and normalises it.

3 *Confidence is sometimes a good proxy for learning.* Normalising self-reflection and the 'why' questions helps build the learner's confidence that they are constantly learning from everything and that no experience was wasted.

4 *Knowledge gain is sometimes a good proxy for learning.* Normalising the process of asking, 'What do I now know about myself?' means that the learner's knowledge of themselves becomes important too.

5 *Remember your definition of success, and make it clear for learners, colleagues, and, if possible, for parents/carers and employers: learners who know where they are and which way they are heading.* Self-aware learners are likely to make better decisions, whatever stage they are in. We would like them all to move swiftly and easily to Action, but a good journey has a longer-term impact on all future journeys than reaching a destination quickly now. Thus, enabling learners to become self-aware through everyone's conversations is a key part of making this happen.

Messages for learners

Knowing myself means knowing what I like and value – and why

Knowing myself means knowing what I can and can't do – and how to do something about it

I can learn more about myself by asking myself, 'And why do I think that?' or 'And why does that matter to me?'

Knowing more about myself will make the decisions about study and work much easier.

Actions

Staff

- Share your Three Stage Careers Journey model with all staff in your school or college
  - Enable everyone to become familiar with the concept
  - Work with them to determine how they can use it in their work
- Develop some simple reflective questions for all staff in your school or college (see above)
  - Help everyone understand the part they can play in supporting learners through conversations.

Parents and carers

- Support parents and carers to have reflective conversations with learners by sharing your Careers learning journey
  - Use the grids in **Activity 2** to show what each stage means
  - Explain how those stages provide reference points when they hear learners talk about what they read, think, or do
  - Explain how the key decision points fit into that journey
- Demonstrate the role that parents and carers can play in supporting the school or college to enable learners to make decisions well *themselves*
  - Introduce a simple range of impactful reflective questions that parents and carers can use when talking with learners about what they read, think, or do
  - Emphasise messaging about making decisions well, as opposed to good/ bad decisions
  - Describe the role that self-awareness plays in making decisions well, and its value to employers
  - Emphasise messaging that all learning supports effective decision-making
- Support parents and carers with short briefings on …
  - How to support learners who are making decisions about qualifications and next steps or going on work experiences
  - How to help them prepare for those decisions or experiences
  - How to ask effective questions
  - How to enable the learner to feel that they own the process
  - What Employability is, how it surfaces from curriculum learning, and its importance to employers
- Share any briefings with parents and carers that you are giving to employers: some of your parents and carers may also be employers themselves who would want to participate in work experience opportunities if they understood better the benefits learners gain.

Employers

- Introduce the Three Stage Careers Journey you are using in your school/college
    - o Use the grids in **Activity 2** to show what each stage means
    - o Explain how work experiences help learners progress through each of these stages
    - o Articulate how reflection and self-awareness play a part in effective decision-making
- Ask employers to share with you how they see the value of self-awareness when they recruit learners and graduates, and ask them to reflect on that when they talk to learners
- Introduce a simple range of impactful reflective questions that employers can use when talking with learners about work and the workplace, as well as about curriculum learning
- Support employers by creating a short one-page briefing that …
    - o Outlines how an interaction between learners and employers fits with the learner's Careers journey
    - o Indicates what kinds of learning gains the learner might get from the interaction
    - o Provides effective conversation starters about how the learner is finding the experience and beginning to identify benefits
    - o Reiterates that all conversations about the experience and how it fits together for the learner can be meaningful.

Context value

In taking this approach to embedding reflection, you are addressing the needs of each learner (Benchmark 3) by establishing a good foundation for reflection across learners' formal and informal interactions. This helps learners gain more value from personal guidance (Benchmark 8). Building a foundation where the learner owns their own learning, and doesn't solely rely on teachers and Careers professionals, also enables them to develop increasingly a reflective mindset in all their Careers and other thinking. That underpins a stable programme of Careers education because reflection is core to good learning (Benchmark 1).

Note

1 If you are bound by the government statutory guidance, this also connects to Benchmark 4 (Linking Curriculum Learning to Careers).

Activity 9: Get data

At this point in the book, **Activity 9** and **Activity 10** either feel like the icing on a very complicated but wonderful cake: worth the time and investment of effort, or they feel like flying to the moon: terrific idea, but I'm not going to do that!

But I have included these activities here because they connect to my wider mission of enabling you to get more impact from what you are already doing. And even if you know you have not got any hope of being able to do these, do have a quick scan through the ideas because the principles behind them are interesting and will help you see the full picture of your other activities.

Data is everywhere. Your learner management systems are full of it, and education technology is dominated by learner analytics. Digital systems for managing and recording learners' progress are now standard, and measuring outcomes is part of the education landscape at all stages. But tracking the Careers learning journey of your learners is something most people have never even thought about, and until 2012 it was not an established part of the higher education Careers landscape either.[1] But as I have noted before in this book, if you know where your learners are – and they know too – helping them to make progress is much easier than if you don't.

Data is also a powerful way for us to make an evidence-based case for something having impact, and the Careers profession has struggled in the past to move through a qualitative justification for our value to a quantitative one. One of the reasons that mechanisms to track learner Career readiness have become so important in higher education is that the only other measure of success is a work or further study outcome after graduation, which Careers services can only lay tenuous claim to enabling. It is impossible to prove beyond doubt that something the Careers service did actually created a positive work or further study outcome. So, data that evidences learners' Career readiness while they are in the university, and which supports Careers professionals to make real-time decisions about which cohorts of students would benefit from which interventions and services, has got to be more valuable for supporting learners than just outcomes data. There are, of course, problematic aspects to learner analytics and they are not discussed here, but currently on balance the benefits significantly outweigh the concerns.

The value of being able to evidence the impact of delivery on learner Career readiness is equally true of school and college environments. And even without the Benchmarks to define a stable Careers programme, you want to be sure that the huge efforts you are putting in are actually making a difference. Just a small amount of thoughtfully collected data can help you do that.

There are two types of data which you could collect that would help with your impact measurement, and to find out what is helping your learners the most:

- Career readiness
- Careers learning gain.

They can be applied consistently across all your communities of learners, or you can apply them selectively to the cohort where you (and they) would most benefit from the findings.

Career readiness

This is the process by which we capture where your learners are on your Three Stage Careers Journey. In higher education, this is typically done at the start of every academic year, where all students are asked a very simple and short list of questions during their course registration process (hence its HE name, 'Careers Registration').

The questions asked in HE typically follow a similar format across all the 100+ universities currently using this approach worldwide (the significant majority in the UK, as well as others in Australia, New Zealand, and Europe):

- Where are you on your Career journey?
- What do you think you want to do after this qualification?
- Have you got any recent work experience that helps you achieve that outcome?
- What sector do you think you want to work in?

Even asking only the first question would give you a huge amount of information about your cohorts most vulnerable to the **Hourglass Phenomenon (Challenge 1)** and **Paralysis (Challenge 3)**: for example, Year 9 learners considering their secondary qualifications, or post-secondary learners thinking about their choices post-tertiary.

Taking this snapshot at a key time – before choices are first introduced, for example – would reveal how much you need to do with teaching staff to make sure learners have got all the information they need. You could then take the snapshot again afterwards to see if you have achieved what you were hoping for. The possibilities are endless, but I suggest keeping to very simple and consistent question and choice formats. This is for two reasons: firstly, so that learners pick up the same messaging each time; and, secondly, so you get consistent mappable data. If you keep measuring different things, you will not get a helpful picture.

It is easy to lose sight of how the process of data collection does more than just give you numbers. While questions like these on Career readiness generate really useful data and insights for you in supporting learners through key decisions, they also send those very specific messages to learners about the importance of taking notice of what is happening. The very value of asking the question and giving a consistent choice of answers plants a tiny seed in the learner's head, that this journey is something they are on already, that it is constant and not surprising or new. It normalises it. And when you have your Careers learning journey well established and visible to learners, it all ties together and you can realise more collective impact.

A very simple format for a basic Career readiness question might look like this:

What stage are you at in your Career planning? (select one)

- I'm uncertain about who I might become and what's out there for me
- I've got some ideas but I need to explore more to decide what's right for me
- I understand myself well and have a plan to put into action for my next step.

These statements correlate directly to the Explore Encounter Embark journey, but you will note that here they are not labelled by their journey stage. That is an optional choice if you want to align this with your wider journey stage messaging.

When you get the data – which learner identifies with which stage – you could then:

- Do some simple filtering and categorisation in an Excel spreadsheet and produce a pie or bar chart of how many learners you have in each stage, for any given cohort
- Look at learners at an individual level, using their stage of Career readiness to inform a personal guidance appointment
- Work with sub-groups of learners with the same Career readiness in a more focused way, rather than a whole year group whose Career readiness might be spread right across the journey
- Use their answers as a conversation starting point: 'When I last asked you about your Career planning you said you had a few ideas. Where do you think you might be now?'

Based on the higher education model, and depending how much time, capacity, data Skills, and enthusiasm you have, you could also ask other questions. For example:

What do you think you might do after completing your Sixth Form/college education? (select one)

- University
- I think I want to go on studying but I'm not sure if university is right for me

- A school leaver programme or degree apprenticeship, combining a degree and study
- An apprenticeship that focuses more on work than study
- A job: I'm not sure what yet but I don't want any more study
- I think I want to start working but I'm not sure what kind of work option to take
- I'm not sure which of these is right for me.

This would generate a lot of information for you about where you need to devote time and resource. Tracking that data year on year, or throughout the year after different Careers activities and interventions, gives you a lot of information you can respond to.

But it does not only have to be used for Career readiness. A very simple format for Year 9 learners might look like this:

How do you feel about making your GCSE choices? (select one)

- I don't know what choices to make
- I have a few ideas but need to narrow them down
- I know exactly which ones I want to do.

As above, the correlation to Explore Encounter Embark should be clear.

Depending on how sophisticated your technology is in terms of how the learner engages with these questions, you could create some routing to navigate learners to different subsequent questions and actions, depending on their initial answers. For example, in the routing of answers and follow-up questions mapped in Figure 16, only the two answers which show uncertainty about GCSE choices lead to further actions (Explore and Encounter), because the Embark learners do not need further support.

I have not put in all the subsequent possible stages that might follow these questions, but you can see the idea. You can then navigate the learner directly to actions they can take, such as meeting a subject teacher, speaking to a form tutor, meeting a Careers professional, reading further information, and so on.

One other question you might ask is about work experience. In the original HE development of this process, Gilworth and Thambar also asked students to identify what work experience they had already gained, and then explored correlation with the stage of Career readiness (see Appendix 1). This question would not be relevant to all your learners in different age groups, but if you wanted to evidence to anyone that work experience has a bearing on Career decision-making, then asking this question, particularly of post-16 learners, might generate some useful data.

It is very likely that you are already triaging learner need in this way, but the data that this approach gives you if you ask the questions like this in a systematic, structured, and cyclically repeated way is incredibly useful for making sure that you have resources ready to respond to where need is. Alongside

Figure 16. Explore and Encounter: Mapping GCSE choices

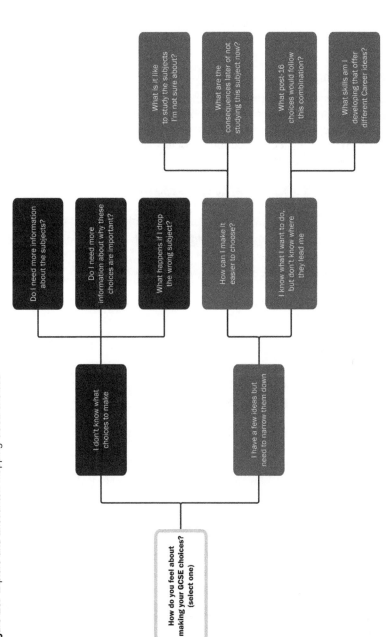

capturing Careers choice, this gives you evidence that your Careers programme is having an impact, and if something has not been as impactful as you hoped, you can then look at how you are presenting your activities to learners (**Activities 3** and **4**) to identify where the issues might be.

Careers learning gain

This is an extension of **Activity 4** and applies **Activity 6** to gather data: we ask the learner not just where they are, but what has changed for them. What is the learning gain to them of engaging with a Careers activity?

In **Activity 6**, I used this example of *Before* and *After* choices for a one-to-one guidance conversation:

Before I attended this personal guidance appointment:

- I felt uncertain about who I might become and what's out there for me
- I had some ideas about what I want to do next, but needed help narrowing them down
- I had a really clear idea of what I want to do next.

After attending this personal guidance appointment:

- I still feel uncertain about who I might become, but I know how to start thinking about it
- I have started to narrow my ideas down and know what other information and experiences I need to access to help me do that
- I now know what I want to do and what steps I need to take next.

If you are using a learner management system or VLE to ask these questions you can access the data readily, or you may just want to keep a spreadsheet. Either way, you can code the learner responses to these questions very simply. Figure 17 shows how you can assign a numerical value to a change of stage on the Careers journey.

Again, a simple analysis in an Excel spreadsheet will generate a chart that shows you what happens to your learners at each stage, and if you replicate this reflective process across different types of delivery, it will help you identify which learners are engaging and feeling the impact, and which activities you offer are giving impact in which stages.

This process is not just for creating pretty charts and tables though. This data is particularly powerful as a way of proving to ourselves (and anyone assessing us from the outside) that we are making a difference. Being able to say, 'The majority of learners who were in Explore before an employer came to speak at the school are now in Encounter' is a really good way of being able to reassure everyone with an investment in this outcome that it is achieving what it should.

Figure 17. Explore Encounter Embark: Measuring learning gain

BEFORE	Value	AFTER	Value	DIFFERENCE
Explore	1	Explore	1	0
Explore	1	Encounter	2	+1
Explore	1	Embark	3	+2
Encounter	2	Explore	1	-1
Encounter	2	Encounter	2	0
Encounter	2	Embark	3	+1
Embark	3	Explore	1	-2
Embark	3	Encounter	2	-1
Embark	3	Embark	3	0

Table design by Kalina Zlatkova. © Kate Daubney 2021.

Key principles for you

1 *Any data you can gather about learner readiness and journey stage will help you find out if you are offering the right services to the right learners at the right time.* It is easy to assume that following the Benchmarks means you are creating a 'stable Careers programme', but even the smallest amount of data can reinforce and evidence that you are doing the right thing for your learners.

2 *If you haven't much capacity to gather and interpret data, keep it simple.* What is the most useful insight to you in terms of being sure your efforts are making a difference?

3 *Try to remain consistent in which data you collect year on year or term on term.* It is easy to get carried away, once you realise what the data offers you! But sticking to looking at the same elements all the time will show you changes and differences in learner cohorts. Patterns in data are more useful than snapshots, particularly for building stability and testing new ideas.

4 *Who is the data for?* Who do you need to convince? Yourself, senior managers, governors, external assessors, employers, parents and carers? Data is evidence, but who can learn and do the most with that evidence?

And don't forget learners: seeing their own learning journey progress is really powerful for them too!

Messages for learners

I know where I was when I started this activity; I know where I am now I've finished it

I can see what has changed for me as a result of doing/reading/engaging with this

I can tell you something I've learned from doing/reading/engaging with this

I can tell you how what I've learned has helped me understand something about myself

I can think about what I can do next.

Actions

- Evaluate your capacity for analysing the data before you start collecting it
  - Basic Excel Skills will go a long way to producing meaningful interpretation
  - There is a bottomless pit of opportunity in data collection and interpretation, so don't collect more than you have the time and energy to look at, otherwise you will miss *your* learning gain!
- Identify what your most effective means are for sharing questions with learners
  - Does your learner management system offer you a platform, or do you need to look for another approach?
  - Ensure that your data is feeding into somewhere you can easily access, download, and interpret it, otherwise you will put off looking at it because there will always be something easier to do
- One of the best things about having data is sharing it
  - Who are you sharing it with?
  - What stories do you want it to tell?
  - How can you tell those stories so that you get the most learner-centred value across?

Context value

In taking this approach to getting data, you are addressing the needs of each learner (Benchmark 3) and ensuring a stable Careers programme (Benchmark 1) by being able to measure the impact of what you do. The more data you gather across different types of activity, the more you can see and demonstrate the relative importance of your different areas of activity to your learner cohorts.

Note

1   See Appendix 4 for information about how this evolved.

Activity 10: Brand

It might seem obvious, but learners (and parents and carers, and colleagues and employers) need to know that Explore Encounter Embark – or whatever you are calling your journey – is the way you map the Career journey in your school or college. If you are going to the trouble of defining this journey, then it needs to infiltrate and shape absolutely every communication and activity you undertake in Careers provision – and possibly some other areas – including:

- Careers programme identity
- Mapping the journey
- Activities
- Events
- Resources
- Learning gains
- External interactions, including employers, alumni, parents, and carers.

'Branding' as a word also seems laden with implicit financial spend, but it starts with:

- Clarity of language
- Consistency in language
- Visibility of language.

Those are factors you can implement for free. Again, if you are going to the trouble of doing this, it has to be done consistently across everything and that begins with proof-reading and careful writing. You do not need fancy graphics to get that part of your approach right.

Design can help, though. You might have a parent or alumnus in your community who could do a simple piece of branding for you. It would also make a great project for a group of learners to design some branding through or alongside their art or design curriculum learning. Either way, involving learners is really important: they need to see the journey presented in a way that is engaging for them, otherwise they will not engage as fully as they might. You might want to illustrate a sense of progress from one stage to the next, or that learning and experiences can be combined in different ways. There is no perfect answer here, but underpinning everything is the need for consistency and accessibility, and thinking like the people you most need to engage: your learners. So, if you start with your journey words, the rest should follow.

A word about justification for branding: for some years I had a long, ongoing argument with a colleague in a marketing role about whether brand was important in Careers activities. There was a prevailing perception that no internal brand should be bigger than the organisation's brand, and that Careers activities did not need marketing to learners. My view, simple though it is, is that there should be nothing more important to an educational organisation than what happens to its learners after they leave, and how they realise the benefit of the education they have received.

That is what the branding of Careers activities and the learning journey is for. It is not for showing off, or being flashy, or rebelling against institutional messaging. It is for making sure that once the learners are through the door, they understand that everyone's goal is enabling them to be successful and realise the value of that success in the longer term, whatever they do. Careers branding is not independent of organisational branding at a conceptual level, even if it looks different. It is an extension of the same message. We are here for you on your journey.

Sometimes learning environments give whole Careers programmes a name, like Advance or Find Your Way. I have seen that done with internships programmes, for example, and these words are generally chosen to be inspiring. But sometimes they indicate our intention for the programme more than the experience as the learner actually sees and engages with it, so such phrases can reflect the thoughts of the Careers professional and not the learner. Sometimes, saying exactly what it is, is the most effective way of guaranteeing it will be well understood, so it can be helpful to bear that in mind.

Key principles for you

1 *Any branding you develop should stem from your Careers journey stage words.* Keeping it simple and consistent is really vital for keeping learners engaged and self-aware. Putting time and thought into generating a limited number of templates at the start saves masses of time later and also helps focus your efforts onto getting the right message across as simply as possible.

2 *If you are branding the journey, make sure it is really visible.* Everything you create or share should have the branding and the same branding used in the same way. Learners should constantly 'bump into it' in all their interactions with Careers professionals, and preferably across the school or college in other ways too.

3 *If you are developing a visual brand, try to involve learners in its development.* Think like the learner matters here as much as in any other part of the provision.

4 *Do not feel challenged if you have to justify the need for the Careers journey and activities to have their own brand.* Keep to a simple message that everyone can agree with. We are here for you on your journey.

Messages for learners

I know what the Careers learning journey stages are

I can see which learning journey stage applies to me right now, and where else I can progress to

When I do/read/engage with a Careers activity or resource, I know how it fits and helps with my journey.

Actions

- Evaluate your capacity for creating a brand before you try to establish one
  - Where will it fit with current branding around Careers and in your school or college?
  - As with data, there is so much you can do, but keep it simple and consistent so learners are always informed and never confused
- Develop a brand that will have some longevity about it
  - You do not want to change your brand every year because learners will be confused
  - So keep it simple and relatively timeless in terms of fonts, colours, or other gimmicks of design
- Plan for all your uses before you get the brand designed, so you know exactly how you are going to use it
  - Any design professional can create a suite of templates for you, but you also want a good idea about the scope of templates you need before you start
  - The journey, learning gains, pull-up banners, posters, event marketing, briefings, information resources are just a few of the areas of activity which you could brand, so map that before you start
- The best bit about having a brand is sharing it
  - How are you getting your brand across to all the people it makes a difference to?

Context value

In taking this approach to developing a brand around your Careers journey, you are reinforcing all the other work you are doing in addressing the needs of each learner (Benchmark 3) and ensuring a stable Careers programme (Benchmark 1). Brand is not essential to making that happen, but it can be the glue that pulls your considerable and diverse efforts together more tightly.

Careers: Summary

I would be the first person to admit that you might be feeling a bit tired having read all the Activities in this section of the book! There is a huge amount that is possible in creating an effective Careers learning environment. That is what we have been focusing on in this section: not just a programme, but creating and sustaining a learning environment where Careers thinking is enabled, takes place, makes sense and is owned by individual learners.

In both of my very different roles as a head of a university Careers service, I frequently felt overwhelmed by the scope and possibility of what you can do. And that is with the benefit of having colleagues and teams around me to help me put ideas into action. I know that for many of you reading this book, it is just you, working on your own. You are the Careers team in your school or college. So, I want to reiterate a few principles that are hopefully familiar by now, but nonetheless still important.

1 **All these Activities are about getting more impact from what you already do.** It is incredibly tempting to think either, 'We could do this, and that, and that thing, and what about this thing …' or, 'Help, we aren't doing enough!' You are the expert in your learning environment. You know better than anyone who your learners are, and where they most need help. You are already doing lots of useful stuff. You are likely not to have the capacity to do very much more, at least not all at once. So which of the Activities could you draw on to make sure that your learners get more benefit from what you are already doing? That is the best way to decide what is and is not worth doing.

2 **Think like the learner.** In schools and colleges it is natural that Careers professionals and teachers are seen as the experts, and also the 'adult' in the room. That subtly prevails when learners are navigated towards choices at key decision-making stages. I think there is a vital role for Careers professionals and teachers in showing the ways forward by establishing what the journey stages look like, when signposting choices that have to be made.

But working with learners as peers is about putting them at the centre of their own Careers learning journeys. We do not plan those journeys for them. We help them create their own. Thinking like the learner is understanding that it is overwhelming, baffling, paralysing, frightening, boring, exciting, never-going-to-happen-to-me. All of those. Probably at the same time. So we hold up the mirror at the right angle at the right time to help learners reflect on themselves, on what different choices mean to them, and what the short- and longer-term possibilities and consequences might be of different decisions that they want to make. Remember, 'There is no such thing as a bad decision; it might just take longer to get to the destination if I take a route that I later decide wasn't quite right for me.' So, which elements of these Activities would most help your learners create and shape their own journeys?

3 **Your measure and definition of success are learners who know where they are, which way they should be heading, and what they need to do to get themselves there.** Reflection is fundamental to this, and clear, simple signposting makes it possible. If you do not do anything else, **Activities 1** and **2** where you map out that Careers journey and make it possible for learners to tell you where they are will reward you again and again.

But reinforcing that message – that going on a self-aware journey is just as important as reaching the destination – will help establish and manage everyone's expectations. We do not cross the same finish line in the same way at the same time. And employers very much want different people working for them, who have different finish lines and arrive there in different ways. Thus, enabling individual ownership of choices is a matter of making decisions well and giving learners the foundation to know how to manage and achieve those choices in the external environment.

I want to stress that 'making decisions well' will lead to 'making good decisions' only if those decisions come from the learner themselves. Schools, colleges, governments, parents, and carers all have their own ideas about what 'good decisions' look like. A good decision for a learner is the one they have made themselves in a fully informed, well-supported fashion, that meets their goals and aspirations now, and forms a sound platform for future decisions, both in itself and in the way that the learner made it. Learning to make decisions well is the lifelong foundation for making good decisions again and again.

Whichever of the **Activities** you decide to try, those three principles should keep you connected to why you are doing it and not just overwhelmed by 'what' you are doing. And just in case I have not stated these enough already, here are the simple messages for learners that sum up everything we have explored in Careers:

I know where I was when I started this activity; I know where I am now I've finished it

There are activities for me, whatever stage of my journey I am at

I know what will change for me as a result of doing/reading/engaging with this

I can tell you something I've learned from doing/reading/engaging with this

I can tell you how what I've learned has helped me understand something about myself

I can think about what I can do next

Part **3**

Employability

I mentioned in the **Environment** section of this book that Employability is not well understood, and that this has become an environmental factor that, in my opinion, has a wide range of negative impacts for learners. These range from the Skills gap oft-mentioned by politicians, business, and in the media, to the **Hourglass Phenomenon** and **Paralysis** I identified in the **Challenges** section. But if we understand it and can talk with confidence about it to learners:

- It gives meaning to qualifications, not just in a specific curriculum context but in relation to their long-term Career choices and mobility
- It joins up having Careers ideas with being able to put them into action
- It joins up qualifications with each other, helping the learner understand themselves and their academic journeys better.

All that contributes to creating and supporting a learner who is self-aware and able to make informed choices about the value of their academic qualifications to their future Careers choices.

The reality is that we ask learners to make academic choices largely in abstract. But practically (as well as morally and ethically in my opinion), that should not happen because qualifications are – in process at least – the gateway to the first big Careers decisions. And yet we separate out academic from Careers choices. Even when we advise 14-year-olds not to give up Chemistry if they want to become doctors, dentists, or vets, we do so because they are factors in a future academic choice of degree programme. We do not generally say, 'You'll need Chemistry, because when you are out in a field trying to diagnose a sick heifer, you will remember everything you ever learned about the organic structure of methane.'

So, in the next section you will find my justification for why Careers and curriculum should be linked and how Employability achieves that, all of which will give your learners the best foundation for a meaningful Career of any type, whatever qualifications they are studying for. You will see research and practice

I have developed to address this, some of which is being shared for the first time in this book.

The origin of that justification emerged because I have been an academic, a teacher, and an educator for all of my professional life, and even though for most of the last twenty years I have also been a Careers professional, it is inescapable that education, qualifications, and Careers are connected in some way. But until now there has not been an effective conceptual or practical exploration of what that really means to learners in practice, and no innovations in technical or vocational qualifications really address the issue.

In the statutory guidance, Benchmark 4: Linking Curriculum Learning to Careers indicates a recognition that this is a feature of learners' experience, but it gives only a limited solution and the Benchmark makes no specific reference to Employability or what it means in this context. The statutory guidance is pretty silent on any wider value of making a connection between curriculum and Careers. Nor does the statutory guidance solve the problem embedded into Benchmark 4 of how teachers might actually achieve linking curriculum to Careers. Nor does it even acknowledge that without an understanding of work-readiness, all the Careers guidance in the world is meaningless and lacks impact.

So even if you are not bound by the statutory guidance, you should definitely read on. Because while this section of the book does show you how to link curriculum learning to careers, that is something you should do because it is possibly the single most useful benefit that we can bring to learners, even beyond a suite of good Careers education activities. In my opinion, turning Employability from something that is entirely alien and misunderstood to something that is embedded into the fabric of our education system is not only absolutely essential, but it is also pretty easy to do.[1]

Because Employability is the wheels on the Careers car. One does not move without the other.

Now, mapping the relationships and benefits that make up Employability is a bit like three-dimensional chess, so the diagram in Figure 18 is not a perfect representation of how this all fits together. The potential for capturing the wider value of Employability is enormous, but I have tried to simplify it sufficiently that you can take this away right now and do something with it. You might or might not share Figure 18 or a version of it directly with your learners, but there is plenty here that you can use in its component parts to help learners understand what Employability is, how they develop it, and what they do with it.

But you should definitely share this way of thinking about Employability with employers and alumni who engage with you and your learners. And in doing so, you will:

- Keep the language of Employability consistent, so everyone knows exactly what they are talking about
- Model self-awareness for learners, supported by everyone talking about their Employability in the same way
- Share language that is simple and easy to understand and re-use.

Figure 18. Employability

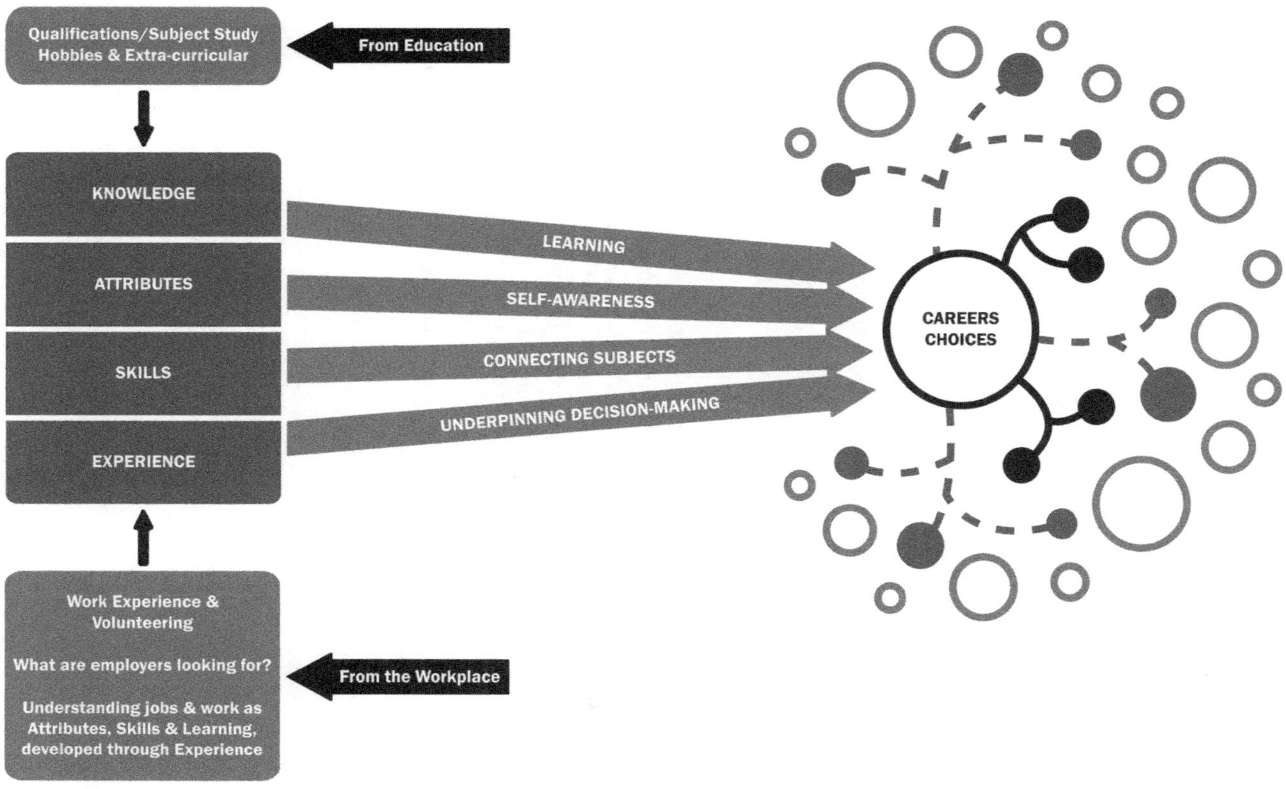

From Education

Qualifications/Subject Study
Hobbies & Extra-curricular

KNOWLEDGE

ATTRIBUTES

SKILLS

EXPERIENCE

LEARNING

SELF-AWARENESS

CONNECTING SUBJECTS

UNDERPINNING DECISION-MAKING

CAREERS
CHOICES

From the Workplace

Work Experience &
Volunteering

What are employers looking for?

Understanding jobs & work as
Attributes, Skills & Learning,
developed through Experience

Illustration by Kalina Zlatkova. © Kate Daubney 2021.

So, do pre-brief speakers on how you want them to present themselves and their narratives when they come to talk about their Careers journeys, and the 'stuff' they picked up on the way to enable them to be successful.

It is also incredibly important to share this way of thinking about Employability with teaching colleagues. This is not only because if you are bound by the statutory guidance, they are the ones on whom the burden of 'linking curriculum learning with careers' often falls, but also because every teacher has had a learner in their class at one time or another who has said, 'What's the point of this? I'm never going to use it after I leave school!' And Employability is the way to answer that question, every single time.

Figure 18 is a diagram that captures Employability:

- what it is
- where it comes from
- what it is for
- how it links to qualifications and Careers choice.

There is a lot going on in that diagram, and I will break it down in the next few sections. But hopefully what you can see already is that Employability is not about any one element. There is no magic bullet that guarantees or enables Careers outcomes. Even a professionally focused university degree like Architecture or Dentistry or an apprenticeship as a Cyber Intrusion Analyst are carefully curated combinations of the four elements on the left that emerge through processes of learning and experience and shape Careers decisions.

This section of the book is in two parts. Firstly, I am going to take you through what Employability is, how it emerges, and how learners develop it, which bits they gain from their environment and which bits start with them. Then, I am going to share a way of looking at the relationship between Employability and academic subject choices that not only addresses the issues created by the current framing of Benchmark 4, but also underpins good Careers decision-making all round.

Note

1   As explained in my Note to Education policy-makers at the start of this book, this is the section I most want you to read. This section makes it very clear which simple but transformational changes can be made, and if you would like me to work with you on doing that, please get in touch. In my research, I have done most of the work for you, you just need to do something with it. You can find my peer-reviewed journal article on this research in the *Journal for Work Applied Management*: full details in Appendix 1.

What is Employability?

Let's start with some definitions:[1]

Knowledge:

- of academic subjects
- of extra-curricular hobbies and interests
- of context: social, cultural, political, economic, etc.

Attributes:

- Qualities (I am ...); Values (I believe in ...); Behaviours (I act to ...)
- Awareness of myself, of others, of context

Skills:

- Specialist
- Transferable

Experience:

- Putting Knowledge, Attributes, and Skills into action
- Gaining and developing Knowledge, Attributes, and Skills.

You can see from Figure 18 that Knowledge is perceived to be the province of school, college, and higher education, while Experience is perceived to be the province of the workplace. That is not the whole story, as we will see in the next few sections, but it is the model that most closely replicates the situation of most learners up to further education and beyond.

There are two more points I would like you to note before we move into the detail, that help show the difference between Careers and Employability. I mentioned these in the first section of this book, but it is worth revisiting them again now because as we explore Employability, the difference between it and Careers will become much clearer. They are often conflated by virtue of being connected. But there are fundamental differences between them.

I noted at the end of **Part 1** that Careers is best demonstrated by a map.

When I get a map, I use it to:

Figure 5. The map

Illustration by Kalina Zlatkova. © Kalina Zlatkova 2021.

- Figure out where I am
- Discover all the places I can get to
- Help me decide which places most interest me
- Learn how to choose my next destination.

This recognises:

- Journeys
- Personal – my choice
- Bespoke – fitted to me.

But we also know that each Careers journey is essentially an iteration of the previous one, carrying learning forward each time a new set of decisions are made. Many Careers theories and models indicate this cyclic progression.

Figure 6. The suitcase

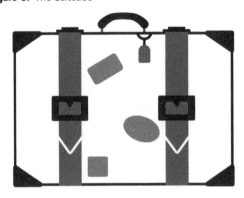

Illustration by Kalina Zlatkova. © Kalina Zlatkova 2021.

Employability is best demonstrated by a suitcase.

When I have a suitcase, I can:

- Figure out what I might pick up on my journeys to put in it
- Decide what I need for different journeys
- Put into it the stuff I accumulate along the way
- Remember that everyone always ends up with more in their luggage than they use!

So this recognises:

- Stuff that belongs to me …
- … which is similar to the stuff that everyone else has
- But it is my stuff that I gather and take on my journeys.

So, that means that Employability is essentially linear, in that it is gained and developed continuously and cumulatively along all of our journeys. We pick up more and more stuff along the way, both at a greater level of expertise and in more diversity.

That also means that while Careers is personal to the learner, Employability is essentially abstract, because everyone can pick up more or less the same stuff on the same journey. The way they use it might be different, particularly in how it underpins their Career choices and outcomes, but it might be just the same Knowledge, Attributes, Skills, and Experience through qualifications, training, and professional development.

I will now explain what I mean when I talk about Knowledge, Attributes, Skills, and Experience.

Note

1 In Appendix 5, I give a short narrative of how I evolved this model and approach. If you have done any research into Employability and read the academic studies I mentioned elsewhere, then you might recognise some of the elements. But what is different about this model, and why it is so useful to learners, is how I evolved it from the existing taught curriculum, the glue that sticks every learner to their future working lives, whichever Careers they choose.

Knowledge

In **Challenge 2**, I suggested that qualifications are principally positioned in our educational culture as Knowledge assets, underpinned by the development of specialist Skills. For example, how to solve a quadratic equation is underpinned by the Skills of algebra. If you read any curriculum documentation for secondary and tertiary qualifications in the UK, the key focus is on the specialist Knowledge and Skills required for the study of the subject. Interestingly, at higher education level, curriculum documentation includes a slightly wider range of reference points around transferable Attributes and Skills (more on that later), but it is not surprising that qualifications there too focus on what you learn in specialist terms that is distinctive to the subject.[1]

We also think about relationships between subjects as commonality in specialist Knowledge: this is why Maths and Physics, History and Politics, Theology and Philosophy, Art and Design, and other combinations are often perceived as linked. Sometimes, one is the foundation of the other in curriculum evolution terms, but synergies are also reinforced by how we position qualification choices to learners: 'If you are studying Physics, you should do Maths as well.' 'History and Politics go well together'

The focus on STEM in Benchmark 4 reinforces this linear perception, because the emphasis on linking curriculum learning to Careers is very direct: it effectively says, 'This Knowledge you learn in your STEM qualifications will be professionally useful to you in a STEM Career'. They might equally have said it about Art or Design, of course, or History for learners who want to become Historians, or Philosophy for learners who want to become Philosophers ...

Ah, but wait a minute ...

You see the problem with this sort of linear thinking! It falls apart immediately you get into a subject area where there appear to be only a tiny number of Career choices that are not directly related to that subject area (professional Philosopher being an obviously rare one outside academic research). Firstly, it cannot be right that linking curriculum learning to Careers is only true when you talk about STEM subjects. And, secondly, it also reinforces the view that Career choices are only possible as a direct linear outcome of subject learning in education. But those outcomes are inevitable when everything we read repeatedly implies that qualifications are principally about Knowledge.

To me, that is just plain wrong. Qualifications are not just about Knowledge: it is just that curriculum is written that way.

And it is also really, really bad messaging for learners.

But we have got ourselves and our learners trapped inside this narrative and while it is not difficult to see where we could be heading instead, a change of course is going to feel like turning the proverbial oil tanker.[2]

So, here are the key messages I encourage you to get across to learners in helping them understand what Knowledge is, what it is for, and how it contributes to helping them not only get their first job, but build lifelong Careers of choice and mobility, if that is what they want.

Knowledge 1: Knowledge is not just about qualifications

Knowledge is constantly gained, all the time, in every single interaction. It is Knowledge of self, of others, of context. Of detailed, precise things like the Arsenal offside trap of the 1980s, the optimum temperature of liquid needed to activate yeast, the exact difference between Country & Western and Americana, or what makes Louboutin shoes recognisably different from Jimmy Choo shoes. Of glacial erosion, titration, Roman civilisation, the French subjunctive, electrons, the model of supply and demand, brush techniques, the firing temperatures of different glazes, woodworking tools, and the biomechanics of throwing the javelin.

Qualifications are full of Knowledge and the specialist Skills that enable learners to apply what they learn. Some of those specialist Skills underpin one subject only (correct use of a surform planer in woodwork), while others underpin many (algebra for Maths, Physics, Chemistry, and Economics).

But jobs and Careers are also full of specialist Knowledge: football is about data and statistics, nutrition and dietetics, anatomy and physiology. Baking is about sustainability, food chemistry, and the physics of cooking. Music is not just rooted in creativity, but is a product of media, image, culture, politics, and society, as well as technology and artisanal crafts of instrument design and manufacture. And shoe design is shaped by physics, textiles, biology, identity, celebrity, media, and the mechanics of the global economy.

Knowledge is also rooted in and a reflection of oneself. One person's Arsenal offside trap is another's Americana. We tend to remember better the things that we are most interested in, and we are most interested in the things that are meaningful to us. If we can understand what defines that meaningfulness for us, why we engage with some things more than others, we can establish good patterns of decision-making that are incredibly useful when choosing Careers and qualifications. I do not think most learners naturally think 'Titration is really fascinating to me, much more so than the French subjunctive.' There isn't the time and space to give learners the chance to unpick why that is the case, nor why they 'get' titration but never seem to grasp the basics of the subjunctive.

And so those often fleeting engagements with Knowledge through curriculum come to form the basis for utterly fundamental decisions that can last an entire lifetime. And that is not very helpful for making decisions well.

The opportunity here is not to try to fix this before we move forward: in our current intense, densely packed educational culture, I do not think it is possible to do that without some sweeping changes in education policy which are hinted at in this book, but currently beyond its scope.

But I think we do have an opportunity to support learners to see that Knowledge is everywhere, and being able to reflect on why something is fascinating or boring is as valuable as the Knowledge itself. And by extension, getting to grips with what Knowledge means to me as a learner can shape how I make lots of other interpretations and decisions.

So, key messages to learners are:

- Knowledge is not just found in qualifications
- I pick up Knowledge all the time both in school/college and beyond it
- Knowledge across both study and non-study interests might give me a platform for choosing Careers I'm interested in
- Taking a minute to think about why some things interest me and why others don't will help me recognise other things I might be interested in later.

Knowledge 2: Qualifications are not just about Knowledge

I have alluded to this already, and I will unpack this in much more detail in the Attributes, Skills, and Experience sections shortly. But if you read any of the secondary and tertiary curriculum for academic subjects (for example, A levels and Scottish Highers), you will see immediately that there is little evidence to contradict the statement that, 'Qualifications are not just about Knowledge'. That seems to be *all* they are about. BTEC curriculum and the T Level curriculums move away from this somewhat, because of the stronger and more explicit professional alignment, providing a bit more focus on some of the more transferable Skills of the workplace, but those subject areas are vocationally or professionally aligned, so you would expect that.

But let us think about that point for a moment: transferable Skills of the workplace. In other words, these are Skills whose relative value to the qualification and the Knowledge is constructed because of, and in justification for, the route into the workplace. Transferable Skills are very much separated from traditional explanations of what Knowledge means. In fact, the standard introduction to BTEC qualifications (in this case, Level 3 Extended National Diploma in Countryside Management (2019), p. 7) recognises:

> Transferable Skills are those such as communication, teamwork, planning and completing tasks to high standards, which are valued in both the workplace and in higher education.[3]

So, we have a sort of division here, which I do not think has been helpful to the perceived difference between conventional academic subjects and those which are more professionally aligned. This division appears to suggest:

- Some qualifications offer Knowledge which then needs more Knowledge to make it useful in the world, but then it still will not be obvious how it might be useful in the world, but that will be sorted out later by someone else who probably isn't an educator ...
- Other qualifications offer Knowledge now which is only useful later in the world beyond education.

Firstly, regardless of whether you are bound by the statutory guidance or not, this gives you an idea of why Benchmark 4 emerged, doesn't it? Because someone thought, 'It isn't obvious to learners why huge swathes of Knowledge gained through many qualifications are going to be useful in the world.' But the statutory guidance solution to that thought is only partial: the emphasis in the background of Benchmark 4 focuses principally on subjects where the Knowledge gained seems more obviously to be useful in the world. In STEM subjects. It does not solve this problem holistically across all subjects equally. And that is just plain wrong.

Thus, you end up with learners taking qualifications who at secondary, tertiary, or higher education level still have no idea how the Knowledge they gained is going to be any use in the world. And what about those learners who have gained Knowledge that they are told is useful in the world ... what if they do not want to go on to use that Knowledge in their Careers?

Oh ... wait. That's exactly the problem we have. For all learners. Curriculum learning positioned as Knowledge. Knowledge which not all learners can equally realise the value of to carry forward into their future Careers.

So, let us not focus only on Knowledge. Let us define 'curriculum learning' differently. Let's figure out what else qualifications offer that open doors to a huge range of future choices, something that is not about the Knowledge that is gained. I do not want a learner who has successfully completed a BTEC in Countryside Management to think that their only Career choice is one in countryside management, any more than I want a Philosophy graduate to think that there is no equivalent role on offer in the job market.

And if you think this is just me being passionate about this, then let me reassure you that one of the biggest and most influential global organisations devoted to economic progress thinks the same way. The Organisation for Economic Co-operation and Development (OECD) has a unit of economists devoted to exploring the role and impact of Skills on global productivity. In their 2019 Skills Outlook, they proposed:

> Enabling life-long and life-wide learning for all is a crucial policy response to changing skills requirements and the uncertainty of future skills needs.[4]

That can only be done if curriculum is changed to increase the focus on high-level cognitive Skills, social Skills, and learning to learn, and that matters as much in schools as it does in supporting and enabling adult learners.[5]

While policy-makers are figuring out how they are going to do that, in the meantime we should help learners understand:

- Qualifications train me for lots of things, including learning specialist information and Skills both in education and in work
- I may not use this particular specialist information or Skills in my future Careers, but I will always know how to get to grips with new specialist information and Skills in future
- Every job requires specialist information or Skills that belong to that job, so I already know how to learn like that
- Qualifications are like a trampoline: I can bounce off them in any direction.

Knowledge 3: Knowledge is just one output of the process of Learning

Lots of very wise and scholarly people, including some very senior managers in universities in the UK, have discussed the essential values of higher education as being:

- The last time in your life that you can really learn for the sake of learning
- The only place you actually learn to learn, rather than simply studying to pass exams.

The educator in me feels that these are two very important principles.
The careers professional in me knows that:

- As we figure out what the world and work look like after a global pandemic crisis, that will shape us for at least a decade if not permanently
- And as in the UK we also wrestle with the economic and social impacts of leaving the European Union, learners will think less and less about those two essential educational principles as motivations for continuing to study post-secondary.

And honestly, I don't blame them.
As one student said to me during a one-to-one appointment not so long ago: 'I love my degree. But what did my £30,000 of tuition fees buy me?' The investment of money – and increasingly of time, in a culture that focuses more on the immediate than the longer term – means that learners want to know what they are getting as a return on their investment.
That said, it has never been more important than now to focus on what it means to Learn rather than just to acquire Knowledge. It is not just a response to the problems of the lifespan or relevance of Knowledge, as I outlined in the previous section. Qualifications are essentially always in the past tense: once gained, they are over, and the Knowledge needs to be continually fed if it is to be maintained or to grow in that area. I think most of us can identify a qualification we once took of which we cannot remember much at all now.

But Learning is about looking at the present and the future. It is not tied to one outcome: it is the underpinning of the possibility of all outcomes. It underpins the mobility of aspirations and ideas, and ultimately of people. Having a mindset that understands the difference between Knowledge and Learning is going to be central to adaptability, whatever the economics, culture, or technology of future job markets.

So, here are three ideas about Learning that are not unique to this book, but I think are more useful to learners than any Knowledge they might ever acquire.

'How to learn is more important than what to learn'

When educators talk about the value of university, these are some examples of why 'how' is more important than 'what'.

- Reading all of Jane Austen's writings – not just *Pride and Prejudice* – to provide context and depth of understanding
- Following Kant down the rabbit hole and back up again into Marxism, to see how ideas evolve and change
- Building on the understanding of DNA to analyse potential treatments for Alzheimer's and expose the possibilities of what is still not known about humans' fundamental genetic identity.

But this is not about becoming an academic researcher. It is only fleetingly about university in a lifetime of work, and university is not a feature of everyone's lives.

But the requirement to learn is constant across all jobs and Careers. It is knowing how to do a job properly, well, effectively, and impactfully, whether it is highly process-based or regulated, or vastly unpredictable and innovative. In our work, each of us is an expert because we have learned and continue to do so. We know things about our work that are not known to others who do not do our work.

It is not just about specific expertise like being a paramedic or concert violinist either. It is organic and evolving. It might be about combining social research from social media platforms with environmental concerns about food production to explore the potential for a new brand of vegan snack. Or about using artificial intelligence to streamline compliance and risk management, replacing the work that graduate entrants into the legal sector used to do with new systems built by the next generation of graduates. It is about interpreting traffic patterns and driver behaviours in real time in city traffic to shape routes and decisions on a bike as a courier or as a taxi driver. It is about exploring how traditional building techniques are complemented by new scientific innovations to create sustainable resources in the construction sector.

Every job requires learning in depth, which requires knowing how to learn as things change. The Knowledge varies, but the requirement to learn does not. Every job is changing in some way: regulatory, environmental, technological, social, economic. And when the job and the world around us change, we have to change too.[6]

Global financial services firm PwC did a huge piece of research about the future of the world of work. Right at the beginning, Blair Sheppard, PwC's Global Leader for Strategy and Research Development says:

> So what should we tell our children? That to stay ahead, you need to focus on your ability to continuously adapt, engage with others in that process, and most importantly retain your core sense of identity and values ... [I]t is not just about acquiring knowledge, but about how to learn.[7]

It has never been more important to move away from seeing qualifications as a static outcome, in and of themselves. Knowledge constantly evolves because learning is what shapes it. To learners, curriculum feels fixed and permanent. But the reality of the world of work could not be further from that. So, let us help learners see that the value of curriculum emerges not in the qualifications themselves, but in the foundation that learning provides for adapting as everything changes.

'Learning Agility is the ability to keep on learning throughout your life'

Having established the importance of knowing how to learn, what do you do with it then? Well, bluntly, you keep on learning; and in some cases unlearning and re-learning. You realise that continuing to learn is important, but also that changing *what* you learn and *how* you learn is also important. It becomes essential as everything around us is also changing. That has strongly surfaced during the pandemic in one simple example, as so many of us learned not only to use meeting technologies and platforms, but also had to grapple with how we learned about, on, and through those platforms: did we use an online VLE, a quick group class with colleagues, reading a manual, looking at the online help resources? But few of us would have thought about anything than learning to do it quickly; we would not have had the capacity to reflect on how our learning agility was being developed. Supporting learners to recognise that now is a valuable insight that will help them.

Likewise, in the latter half of the twentieth century, ways of engaging and learning evolved extraordinarily quickly. We did not need an expression like 'digital native' before the 1990s, and yet now it has become a proxy for an agile mindset when compared to a 'digital immigrant'. More recent and appropriate conceptualisations like 'digital visitor' and 'digital resident' might reflect more accurately how the internet is the environment within which digital residents primarily engage with each other. But a different way to look at this overall is the distinction between 'What tool do I need to do this?' and 'What can I do with this tool?'

Either is, in practice, a reflection of Learning Agility: the understanding that wherever you are starting from, you will need to learn something new either to get to the outcome you want to get to, or to map all the outcomes you might be able to get to. In the workplace, it is seen as the ability to figure out what to do when you do not really know what to do. In corporate contexts, Learning Agility is highly sought after because it encapsulates the ability to achieve results in rapidly changing environments. If you are familiar with the acronym VUCA – Volatile, Uncertain, Complex, Ambiguous – you will be aware that this is now a very common concept for capturing constant change through these four elements.

So, Learning Agility combines the ability to change your approach and perspective with the ability to deliver outcomes, bring other people with you, and manage change. All of that – unsurprisingly – is much easier if you know yourself well, because you can see what adjustments you need to make to yourself first.

As with the OECD's Skills Outlook reports, the World Economic Forum's Future of Jobs annual reports are an interesting read. As long ago as 2016, the WEF was suggesting that, 'incentivizing lifelong learning' and 'wholesale reskilling' should be a global priority.[8] But contributions to their more recent global summits include discussion of 'de-learning' and 'unlearning': individuals let go of what they already know in order to learn new Knowledge and Skills in new ways, opening up new perspectives, ideas, and solutions.

The way that we have always looked at the linear journey through education to work will be fundamentally changed by this rapid increase in the rate of disruption created by all this upheaval. And school, college, and university education cannot remain immune to this shift of emphasis while the working world evolves rapidly. In the WEF's 2018 report, they proposed that between 2018 and 2022, an average timeframe of just over 100 days would be required to reskill workforces towards what was required.[9] The timescales of global education systems cannot remain on their current rigid patterns if the timescales of the workplace are going to be so different.

Now that might all seem pretty terrifying. So what part can we as educators play in supporting learners into their future Careers and to support their developing Employability? I think the message is about as simple as the context might seem terrifying: let's encourage learners to maintain an awareness of, and focus on, their own learning. Do not be frightened by change: look on it as an opportunity to let go of some things and try others. Focus on how you learn and not what you learn. Keep being flexible about learning and interested in learning, throughout your life. If you keep doing that, you will be able to explore and embrace opportunities as they arise.[10]

'Know it all' is replaced by 'Learn it all'

Much of what I have referred to in this section, let alone this book, has reflected a need to see things differently. Education systems are largely a fixed structure, but even without the constant context of change, effective learning is embedded in a mindset that says 'What can I do next?' Carol Dweck's influential book *Mindset* has framed this concept as what she calls the 'growth mindset' and is worth a read in itself. But the key interpretation in relation to Careers and in particular to Employability is that Knowledge is a fixed asset, while Learning is about growth: a noun as opposed to a verb, if you like. Furthermore, I think Careers and Employability can both be seen as reflections of a growth mindset: things will change, so what can I do that will enable me to learn as I go along and support the decisions I will need to make?

It is inescapable that learners have Knowledge, and it is a valuable asset in and of itself, particularly if a learner does want to become a vet and draw on Chemistry, or use algebra to model economic growth in South America, or apply effective brush techniques and appropriate glazes to decorate sustainable bamboo tableware. But the qualifications system that we have only measures what is known; it is not designed to push learners to demonstrate their ability to learn (or even to unlearn). That is an expectation of the workplace and, as a result, in my opinion, we are making it incredibly difficult for learners – and the employers who eventually recruit them and have to teach learners to do this – to jump across that gulf from the acquisition of Knowledge to the daily engagement, development, and application of their learning Skills.

There is a brilliant, if somewhat ironic, example of the difference between 'Know it all' and 'Learn it all' in our own profession. When they start their training, Careers guidance professionals often say that the aspect of the role they are most concerned about and fear mastering the most is getting to grips with labour market information. What jobs are out there, what do individuals need to get into different sectors, what's the right experience, where are the growth sectors and what's in decline, and so on. I recognise this very profoundly myself: when I started as the PhD Careers Adviser at the London School of Economics, my very first client told me in advance that they wanted to move into investment banking after completing their social sciences PhD. I knew nothing about investment banking, and I spent two exhausting days before meeting them trying to read everything I could get my hands on. I was absolutely paralysed by the idea that I would not know enough to support that student in that conversation. Barely three weeks after that first appointment Lehman Brothers collapsed, permanently changing the landscape I had worked so hard to navigate. Now imagine a scenario where you do not know who is going to walk into the appointment room on any given day. How can you prepare to make sure you can answer any and every possible question you might be asked?

Of course, you are not going to do that. You are not even going to think of trying to do that. I do have incredibly able colleagues who read like sponges, absorbing endless information and statistics and are able to reproduce them on demand. I am not one of those people. And actually, even if you can hold onto detail like that, you cannot possibly stay on top of all the details of all the possible Careers and labour markets.

But what you are going to do, without fear or loss of confidence, is sit down with the student and say, 'How can *we* learn what *you* want to know?' You are going to apply what you already know, and see where it takes you. You are going to draw on your Knowledge in a different way by applying how you learned it, looking through each door it might open and responding accordingly. You will act on each piece of information you find in an agile way, to enable the student to draw their own value from it. You are also going to learn something, alongside the student. But while the student will probably want to remember that information to form the basis of their Careers thinking, what you will remember is how to source that information, and how agile you were in using it to take the next step each time. You are not seeking to 'Know it'. You are demonstrating how to 'Learn it'.

This connects to my earlier point about 'unlearning'. History is littered with examples of discoveries that relied on someone saying, 'What if that thing I thought was true isn't true any more?' Unlearning is not about completely forgetting everything you knew and rebuilding everything from zero. But it is about saying, 'What if I let go of the ways I originally learned about this and what to do with it? What if I put that to one side for a moment and let my imagination explore? What if things I always thought were different and separate can connect in a way I never saw them connect before? And let's see what happens ....'

Higher education is more focused on developing learning than school and college education, though learners often enter university with the perception that they are going to learn everything: in other words, heap Knowledge on top of more Knowledge. Anyone with experience of higher education knows that isn't true: it is more about what you choose not to learn, what specialisms you choose over others you discard, and about how deep down into the subject you want to go. Depth is definitely emphasised over breadth, the longer the higher education continues. But that depth does include more expectation on the learner to apply what they have learned to try different approaches and solve new problems, than simply to repeat it. Nonetheless, a higher education is defined principally by Knowledge: and if you read any of the standard national curriculum documentation, that is immediately clear.

So, I think the most powerful way to support learners who are entering work is to help them understand that learning in the workplace is not very much like qualifications-based Knowledge-assessed education in school and college. The workplace is a very live environment, with constant opportunities to do what we know how to do, but also to approach things in different ways, solve new problems, and explore stuff we do not already know. It is about learning new ways to apply what we know, and learning stuff we do not know. I think for many learners who feel trapped by curriculum as a rigid qualifications-bound experience, that might seem exciting and different and interesting if we can portray it that way.

* * *

I have shared some fairly philosophical thoughts in this chapter about what it means for us as educators and careers professionals to work with learners at the transition between education and work, particularly in terms of how we talk about Knowledge and how learners understand the purpose of Knowledge. So, firstly, Figure 19 is a diagram that I hope pulls it all together:

Figure 19. Knowledge, qualifications, and learning

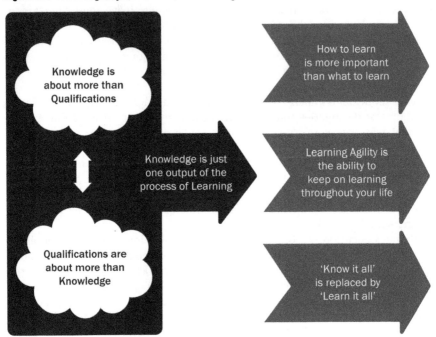

Illustration by Kalina Zlatkova. © Kate Daubney 2021.

Here are some **Activities** for you to explore these ideas with learners:

- Introduce Employability by talking about Knowledge and Learning
  - What is the difference between Knowledge and Learning?
  - What kinds of Knowledge are required to do a job?
  - What are the key changes or factors that might influence how a job evolves, and when new Learning would be required?
  - What Knowledge do learners already have that might be useful in different roles?
- Evaluate job descriptions for Knowledge and Learning
  - What Knowledge requirements can learners find? (e.g. What is the applicant expected to know already?)
  - What Learning requirements can learners find? (e.g. What will the applicant be expected to learn to do? What training will be provided?)
- Scenario discussions for different roles
  - What Knowledge would be essential for doing this role?
  - What might change in this job require Learning to do new things?
- Scenario discussions for Learning
  - What does Learning something new feel like? (rewarding, exciting, challenging, scary, brain-freezing, etc.)

- What does being successful at Learning mean to the learner? (change, mastery, satisfaction, pride, opportunity, etc.)
- What examples can the learner give of a time when they found Learning something new to be fairly easy? (can be extra-curricular)
- What examples can the learner give of a time when they found Learning more challenging? (can be extra-curricular)
- Talk to teaching colleagues in your school or college about how Knowledge and Learning fit into Employability
  - What support can you give them in their teaching and interactions with students to connect academic study to Employability?
  - What can you learn from their teaching activities to help connect academic study with Employability for learners?

Messages for learners

Knowledge is not just about qualifications:

I pick up Knowledge all the time

Knowledge across both study and non-study interests might give me a platform for choosing a Career I'm interested in

Taking a minute to think about why some things interest me and why others don't will help me recognise other things I might be interested in later.

Qualifications are not just about Knowledge:

Qualifications train me for learning specialist information and Skills

I may not use this particular specialist information or Skills in my future Career, but I will always know how to get to grips with detail and master it

Every job requires specialist information or Skills that belong to that job

Qualifications are like a trampoline: I can bounce off them in any direction.

Knowledge is just one output of the process of Learning:

How to learn is more important (and will give you more long-term value) than what to learn

Learning Agility is the ability to keep on learning throughout my life

'Know it all' is replaced by 'Learn it'

Try to stay aware of my own use of Knowledge and Learning: when am I using something I already know? And when am I drawing on (or abandoning) what I know to learn something new?

Notes

1 I admit now that this is probably the most philosophical section of the whole book. I feel very strongly about the content in this section, but after a few paragraphs, you may not feel the same way! So, if you can't face me unpacking what I think are some of the most fundamental issues facing our role at the transition between education and work, then at the end of the Knowledge section you will find a brief summary of the key messages for learners. And you can jump straight there and then move on!

2 Again, if you are an education policy-maker and you have got this far, please keep reading. I promise you I know how to turn the oil tanker.

3 There is an irony here that most learners do not enter higher education knowing that those Skills are valued, expected, or going to be developed further; nor do most higher education institutions present that value as part of the learning gain on offer.

4 *OECD Skills Outlook 2019*, p. 232.

5 Senior Economist Glenda Quintini leads work in this area and her blog is worth a look: details in Appendix 1.

6 In Appendix 1, you can find reference to a public policy research paper I contributed to on this issue.

7 PwC (2018) *Workforce of the Future: The competing forces shaping 2030*, p. 4. Available at: https://www.pwc.com/gx/en/services/people-organisation/publications/workforce-of-the-future.html (accessed 29 January 2021).

8 World Economic Forum. *The Future of Jobs: Employment, Skills and Workforce Strategy for the Fourth Industrial Revolution 2016: Executive Summary*, p. 8. Available at: http://www3.weforum.org/docs/WEF_FOJ_Executive_Summary_Jobs.pdf (accessed 29 January 2021).

9 World Economic Forum. *The Future of Jobs Report 2018*, p. 19. Available at: https://www.weforum.org/reports/the-future-of-jobs-report-2018 (accessed 29 January 2021).

10 Higher education has often been considered relatively unagile and slow to evolve. The pandemic has forced many global higher education institutions to reposition learning online but now learners themselves appear to be struggling to become agile about what they see as a loss of a unique campus-based learning experience. We cannot be sure what the future holds, so in my opinion the Attributes, Skills, and Experience gained from learning in this new way will become an incredibly valuable foundation for the future, even if it feels at the moment that something hoped for is lost.

Attributes

Employability is littered with terms that people use in different ways, and Attributes might be one of the most confusingly named and widely misunderstood of all of them. You might have come across 'personality traits', 'aptitudes', or 'soft skills' (I hate that last expression with a huge passion, see below!)

The Oxford English Dictionary defines Attribute as:

> *n.* quality ascribed to person or thing; material object recognized as appropriate to person or office; characteristic quality

Skill, on the other hand, is defined as:

> *n.* expertness, practised ability, facility *in* an action or *in* doing or *to* do something; dexterity

So describing qualities as practised abilities, which are then 'soft', implying that they are somehow less valuable, significant, relevant, or pertinent than a 'hard skill' (whatever that might be), is – in my opinion – imprecise, inaccurate, inappropriate, and misleading.[1]

Furthermore, many of our most significant roles in society, such as in the healthcare professions, require characteristic Attributes of personality above any one skill: compassion, curiosity, open-mindedness, patience. You cannot do those roles without having, developing, and nurturing such Attributes.

As noted earlier, I define Attributes as being one of three elements:

- I am ... – Qualities
- I believe in ... – Values
- I act to ... – Behaviours

Another way of looking at them is that Attributes stem from awareness of myself, of others, and of my context. So, self-awareness is fundamental in identifying one's Attributes, exploring the ones we do not use much and the ones we might want to develop further or explore for the first time.

This is not a psychological or neuroscientific book, so I am not going to get into the brain chemistry of changing behaviour. Carol Dweck's *Mindset* and Sarah-Jayne Blakemore's *Inventing Ourselves* both tackle this with professional and academic credibility, but my experience of working with learners for almost thirty years suggests that Attributes are both innate, and can emerge to be developed and enhanced. Hence my earlier reservations about psychometric testing of learners as part of Career exploration: if you tell a learner that they do not have the right Attributes to follow a particular Career path, you are denying them the chance to explore if they want to and can evolve the Attributes and Skills to do so.[2]

I think it is true that some of these Attributes might require a learner to develop more than others would: as educators we have all worked at one time or another with learners who appear to lack curiosity, empathy, or open-mindedness, for example. But exposure to different experiences and opportunities can help a learner see something in others that they can then learn to develop in themselves. Hence the role of self-awareness in both developing Attributes and in good Careers decision-making. And hence, again, the importance of reflective opportunities.

Personal, Social, and Health Education (PSHE) syllabuses offer a lot of content reflecting identification and development of Attributes across all Key Stages in the UK education system, but in practice many Attributes also emerge in academic curriculum too. For example, flexibility and adaptability are central to the study of Philosophy or literature in exploring different points of view; engaging interculturally is fundamental to History and Geography, as well as Languages; curiosity is fundamental to sciences, and an innovative mindset is core to any of the creative disciplines and Physical Education, and so on.

However, as we will discover when we look at transferable Skills in the next section, Attributes are not commonly surfaced in school and college curriculum, and they can be relatively more difficult to find in higher education curriculum too. But when you see a list of them, it becomes really obvious that these are exactly the same elements that employers put in job descriptions:

We are looking for someone enthusiastic, personable, and energetic ...

The role holder will need to be highly self-motivated, committed, and focused ...

Typically this job requires a lot of independence, taking the initiative, and remaining calm under pressure ...

And because for learners of school and college age Attributes more obviously seem to surface when they do things outside the curriculum – through hobbies and interests as well as innately to personality – they are often the elements that learners with limited or no work experience can seize on to show their suitability for work. Because if Attributes are innate to the learner, then the learner is already bringing something valued or required to the role.

So, Attributes can be a brilliant starting point for helping learners to understand Employability.

One of the reasons that Attributes get called 'soft skills' is because an Attribute that is a Behaviour (I act to ...) might also be seen as a skill (I do ...). The distinction I am making here is that an Attribute starts with the individual, whereas a skill starts with an external requirement. For example:

I (act to) take the initiative ... (because I want to make a difference and see what is possible)

I (do) take the initiative ... (because otherwise the customer is going to be standing there waiting for someone to solve the problem for them).

Likewise, 'I am focused' could be seen also to mean, 'I have got good organisation and time management Skills'. And, 'I am personable' could be seen also to mean, 'I have got good relationship-building Skills.'

I will admit it is not a perfect science: it is actually a wonderfully messy thing because of language and nuance and individual interpretation. But I think we can easily enable learners to see that an Attribute is a quality, value, or behaviour that *they* bring because of what *they* think is important, whether that is innate to them or something they find they need to develop. Of all the Employability elements, it is the one that most obviously starts with and belongs to the learner.

But given that this is the most personal – and arguably the most subjective – element of Employability, Attributes have almost a greater need to be demonstrated through evidence, just as you would for any other element of a job description. Enabling learners to be able to give examples of ways in which they demonstrate different Attributes is really important, and you can also use examples of different qualities, values, and behaviours to introduce learners to what we mean by Attributes, and start them thinking about how they demonstrate that they have different ones.

Figure 20 provides a short list of different kinds of Attributes to draw on.

Just as self-awareness is important in Careers decision-making, so it is essential in developing Employability too. Reflecting on Attributes is a good place to start younger learners thinking about Employability, without even

Figure 20. Attributes

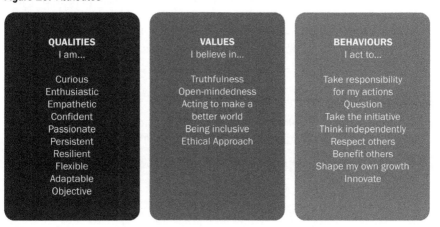

QUALITIES I am...	VALUES I believe in...	BEHAVIOURS I act to...
Curious	Truthfulness	Take responsibility
Enthusiastic	Open-mindedness	for my actions
Empathetic	Acting to make a	Question
Confident	better world	Take the initiative
Passionate	Being inclusive	Think independently
Persistent	Ethical Approach	Respect others
Resilient		Benefit others
Flexible		Shape my own growth
Adaptable		Innovate
Objective		

Graphic by Kalina Zlatkova. © Kate Daubney 2021.

using the 'E word'. It is never too soon to help learners understand that knowing who you are is fundamental to making decisions well at each stage: about what to aim for, what to apply for, and what defines success for you.

Activities for you

- Introduce Employability by talking about Attributes
  - Attributes are personal and innate to the individual
  - Attributes can also be grown and developed
  - Attributes appear in every role and every job description
- Scenario discussions for different roles
  - Which Attributes would be useful for doing this role?
  - What examples can the learner give of a time when they demonstrated that quality, value, or behaviour?
- Scenario discussions for different Attributes
  - What kinds of situations are there where one specific Attribute would be important?
  - What examples can the learner give of a time when they demonstrated that quality, value, or behaviour?
  - What kinds of roles or Careers exist where those situations might arise, or where that Attribute would be important?
- Evaluate job descriptions for Attributes
  - Which ones can learners find?
  - What examples can the learner give of a time when they demonstrated that quality, value, or behaviour?
- If you have pastoral tutor or form tutor roles in your school or college, share these activities for their discussions with learners
- Share lists of Attributes with teaching colleagues to give them Employability language to use in academic study
  - For example, problem-solving can be as much about persistence and patience as being highly skilled at solving the problem
  - And being objective is a really important part of stepping outside a novel to see what the themes are, and finding different interpretations of the author's intentions.

Messages for learners

Attributes – I am … I believe … I act to … – are a great way for me to learn about Employability and what employers are looking for

When I talk about my Attributes, it is helpful to have some examples:

– What evidence do I have that I am enthusiastic?

– Can I describe a project where my time management was really good?

– When was I calm under pressure?

Even if I've never had any work experience, my Attributes are something that employers want

I already have some Attributes: knowing what they are will be really helpful for making good decisions about future work or study

I can develop new Attributes: if there is a quality, value, or behaviour I don't currently have but is important for a Career I want, I can develop it by learning from experience and from others

Understanding which Attributes are important in which situations and Careers will help me make good decisions and use my Attributes effectively and impactfully for my own benefit and that of others.

Notes

1 I am not the only Careers educator to think this. Dr Farouk Dey, a leading American Careers education scholar and practitioner, proposes 'soft skills' should be renamed 'success skills'. See the Appendix for reference to his article.

2 Carol Dweck talks extensively in *Mindset* about the risks attached to having a fixed mindset, particularly in an educational context. In my experience of working with many learners, psychometric testing that produces Career outcomes reflecting learner inputs reinforces the possibility of the learner's view of themselves remaining fixed: 'These are my outcomes'. That is not good for Career exploration or, as Dweck argues, for developing potential. See Appendix 1 for reference details for her book.

Skills

Mind the gap

'Skills' is possibly the most overused word in policy, government, education, and the media when it comes to talking about the workplace and, in particular, transition into the workplace. A narrative has emerged which reinforces the view that Skills are highly differentiated by their role in employment, making them separate from education. The narratives around the 'Skills gap' that have dominated for several decades have only added to that, and while there is no dispute that in some specific areas of specialist Skills – in technology, industry, science, and engineering – the UK may not have enough learners or workers with profiles to fit the need, I think 'Skills gap' has been used as a convenient phrase to cover a highly variable picture. I also believe that the gap is not as big as it is perceived across the board, and in this section I will show you why that is the case.

The economic narratives that have emerged during the pandemic have also emphasised the role that digital Skills – as a holistic but somewhat undefined set – have in skill development, particularly for pre-18 learners. The dominance of the digital and virtual world in our daily pandemic and lockdown existence reinforces that these are non-negotiable for future survival. We need to come quickly to terms with the reality that the pandemic is likely to have accelerated the Fourth Industrial Revolution, because of the increased emphasis on virtual and digital tools and interactions. That is not solely about artificial intelligence, and we will probably see some unanticipated and more creative developments as well as the march of automation in the innovations and businesses that emerge in the coming years. I will talk in a later chapter about digital Skills and the transition to work.

During the pandemic, there has become one other really significant reason why we need to understand this particular aspect of curriculum learning differently. With the ongoing and sustained disruption to examinations for pre-18 learners, there are highly prevalent narratives about lost opportunities for these learners to prove themselves. It is true that one way of demonstrating that they have gathered and understood Knowledge has been lost, particularly if that is what examinations are seen to be for.

But the development of Skills that begins at school and continues throughout working life is ongoing and continuous. And examinations are, in practice, a very limited way to demonstrate transferable Skills. If forms of curriculum assessment gave learners more diverse ways to articulate and demonstrate their Knowledge gain *and* their transferable Skill development in a self-aware and comprehensive fashion, then examinations would cease to be dominated by proof of Knowledge gain, and learners could be confident that nothing was lost, and everything was carried forward. It is somewhat nihilistic to allow and enable learners to believe that subjects act as dead end streets if they are not continued lifelong.

When I stopped Physics after A Level, I did not stop modelling and solving problems, or demonstrating my curiosity about how things fit together. I went on to develop those Skills further in my combined degree in Maths and Music. So if we look at the phases of education as part of a longer journey of continuity, growth, and expansion of transferable Skills, and we remove the hourglass narrative about loss and removal of Knowledge, the Skills gap is immediately narrowed because learners enter each new stage of study or work with an anticipation of how what they have already gained will continue to grow, and they will have a readiness and recognition of new Skills to be developed.

Skills: What and what for?

As my comments about 'soft skills' showed in the Attributes section, I think being clear about what we mean when we talk about Skills is fundamental to enabling learners to understand how their education prepares them for work.[1] So, in this section I am going to use these definitions, and hopefully you will see why they are helpful to learners:

Specialist:

- These are the Skills which arise from and are required to be proficient in a particular activity – in academic study, work, hobbies, interests
- They are largely used in that context or in directly related contexts
- They might include use of specialist equipment or software
- Examples might include Skills of dissection, welding, programming an app, speaking a foreign language, a cover drive in cricket, making rya knots in weaving, or singing falsetto
- *Specialist Skills are sometimes also called Technical Skills, but that can imply a limited context, so Specialist is more inclusive.*

Transferable:

- These Skills arise in multiple contexts
- They are used and applied across multiple contexts in similar ways but perhaps with contrasting outcomes
- They do not require specialist equipment or software, but might be used in conjunction with other transferable Skills in different ways

- Examples might include building relationships, planning, making a decision, identifying choices, contrasting different points of view
- *Transferable Skills are sometimes also called Generic Skills. 'Generic' is often used to imply unspecific or even bland, and by extension immovable; 'Transferable' imbues Skills with purpose and action, and is a closer reflection of their actual value and use.*

Specialist and transferable Skills are also used in conjunction with each other, for example:

- Making a decision about how to express a question in a foreign language
- Planning the order in which to programme an app
- Analysing which cricket shot is the right one to play.

There are two specific challenges that learners have when it comes to Skills:

1 Learners are not aware of how many transferable Skills arise and are developed through their academic subject study
2 Learners lack a rich and varied enough language to describe the Skills they have and want to develop.

A great example of the second point is when people talk about 'communication Skills'. I always ask, 'Which ones?' In my research into Skills and curriculum, I surfaced almost thirty different Skills from pre-18 curriculum, and almost sixty different Skills from higher education curriculum that I have categorised as communication. But how many of us automatically identify even ten or twenty when we talk about communicating? So, it is no wonder that if we struggle, learners struggle too.

But the core fabric of workplace activity is Skills, both specialist and transferable, that are used to gain, develop, and apply specialist workplace Knowledge. In the workplace:

- Specialist Skills are either brought by the learner into the role (e.g. coding Skills taken into a user experience design role, or guitar Skills taken into a band) or they are developed in the role
- Transferable Skills and the potential to develop them are brought into the role by the learner, where they continue to evolve, and new transferable Skills will be developed through work.

How do we address these two challenges learners have when it comes to Skills, and how do we enable them to understand better the readiness for work they already have through their academic learning? In other words, how do we help them articulate the Skills value of their education?

Qualifications develop more than Knowledge

In the Knowledge section, I discussed at length the impact of the existing focus on qualifications as Knowledge assets. That perspective has concealed how much development of transferable Skills also takes place in everyday curriculum teaching and learning. But curriculum is not written to demonstrate that – for teachers or for learners – and so that aspect of development that is constantly taking place is never properly articulated to learners. I genuinely do not think many teachers are aware of the scale of Skills that they are developing in their learners either, or if they are, they perhaps do not have the capacity to articulate that alongside all the other expectations on their delivery. Fundamentally, we do not talk about curriculum in that way. Thus, it is no surprise that if Skills are seen to belong in the workplace, and not to be developed in school and college, everyone perceives there to be a gap.[2]

But as I noted earlier in this book, employers in the majority of cases do not employ school and college leavers and graduates on the basis of their accumulated Knowledge. Employers know that:

- School and college leavers and graduates generally will not have specific specialist experience in their Career of choice
- School and college leavers and graduates are trained learners, who can learn new Knowledge and develop new transferable and specialist Skills
- School and college leavers and graduates do have Attributes and transferable Skills that make them suited to different kinds of roles
- Those Attributes and transferable Skills indicate the potential to develop.

Furthermore, if the majority of employers are not looking for school leavers or graduates of particular subjects, they must be expecting to find learners have the Skills they want from across a range of subjects and subject combinations. In **Challenge 2**, I asked:

Why did one global business recruit more graduates of History to become Tax Auditors than from any other subject?

It is time to answer that. If you have studied History at any point, take a minute to think about it. And for the rest of us, here are some questions to get you started:

- Historians often use evidence and original documents: what Skills do you need to sift through those?
- Historians often read different accounts of the same events: what Skills do you need to analyse those?
- What might Historians do with the conclusions drawn in those different accounts?

So, Historians develop a huge range of transferable Skills from studying History. These include:

- Forensic attention to detail
- Find primary sources of evidence
- Manage and organise large amounts of evidence
- Dig deep into evidence to find the most relevant pieces
- Identify which evidence is important for different arguments or points of view
- Compare and contrast different points of view
- See things from different points of view
- Synthesise a narrative by connecting evidence and information
- Write and present narratives in compelling ways.

And that is exactly what Tax Auditors also do. They need to bring a forensic attention to detail to looking through huge volumes of evidence, sifting out which information is important. They can differentiate between sources and synthesise a narrative or trail through evidence to identify cause and effect. That is why Historians make great Tax Auditors – as do students of many other subjects that have similar or partially similar transferable Skill profiles.

But curriculum is not designed at school, further or higher education levels to be described to learners in that way. It is not a question of making a case for History as a gateway to any particular Career. But it is a matter of surfacing the transferable Skills that emerge innately in the discipline in a very visible way to learners. Learners do not realise that these are the Skills that they have as Historians. Nor can those who are also studying English Literature or Chemistry or Music tell you where the commonalities are between those academic subjects, or where and how they are developing more diverse transferable Skills across a combination of subjects.

I also want to be very clear that this is not a matter of how the subject is taught or learned. I have been asked many times when I have presented on this work to teachers and Careers educators whether these transferable Skills only surface in how a learner is taught a particular subject. Certainly the style of teaching and learning will influence the extent to which a learner realises these are the Skills they are developing. A learning style where students have to reflect on and perhaps actively share their experience of working with primary source material as a Historian will give them a better chance of figuring out that they are developing the Skills associated with that. By contrast, learners who experience a traditional didactic style of teaching may be told that these are the Skills but may never explore that for themselves in the practice of the subject and so not develop them fully.

A while ago, I had a conversation with a Chemistry teacher who could not see that the study of the subject, the lab work, and paper-based problems were innately developing in learners an enormous range of transferable Skills in theoretical and practical problem-solving using quantitative and qualitative Skills, evidence-based argument and evaluation of risk, and Attributes in persistence, tolerance for ambiguity, and diligence. Nor could that teacher see that these were the Attributes and Skills that Chemistry students and learners would be using outside the lab in hundreds of different ways. We are not just training Chemistry students to become Chemists and Chemical Engineers. We are training them to be airline pilots and computer engineers and chefs and aid workers and politicians and anaesthetists and potters and brewers and shoe designers.

I think all that can be a slightly terrifying realisation, for teachers and for learners. If we come to terms with the idea that, in many cases, employers are not seeking particular subject combinations in future employees, then it is effectively open season. Anything is possible! And that is **Paralysis by Possibilities**.

Yet there are still some fairly traditional views about which subjects 'go well together'. There is still a significant level of unease when learners choose combinations like Drama, Physics, and French, which are perceived to be unusual. If we are not situating ourselves and our learners in clear channels of arts and sciences, or if we are only comfortable with 'approved' combinations like Maths and Music,[3] what do we say to learners when they follow our other advice of 'Do what you love'? Is that conditional? 'Do what you love so long as it makes academic sense?' We need to redefine academic sense, because the current concept is not fit for purpose. And shortly, I will share some evidence as to why that is the case.

So, having already suggested that curriculum should be thought of as a breeding ground for a huge range of transferable Skills and Attributes, I also want to suggest that learners would benefit enormously from seeing how these Skills and Attributes relate to each other across the whole map of subjects. Why do Drama, Physics, and Geology work well together? Similarity? Not obviously. But they do have a common Skillset. And what about complementarity? Yes. And why shouldn't they combine effectively on that basis alone? Why not encourage learners to see that they will derive enormous short-term enjoyment and lifelong professional benefit from developing a range of analytical, modelling, creative, and communication Skills at the same time? If they can talk about the complementarity of their interests and enjoyment, and articulate the spread of their Skill development, then employers are going to be highly motivated to employ someone with that level of self-awareness.

By doing that we are helping learners see their curriculum not just as clusters, often separate, of Knowledge. But instead to see curriculum as networks of Skills and Skills relationships.

So, what does that look like in practice?

Extracting Transferable Skills from Curriculum: The SkillsMap®[4]

I have made an in-depth analysis of every A Level curriculum currently approved by the UK Government, and cross-referenced to other UK nation qualification systems.[5] I focused on traditional academic curriculum rather than vocationally aligned qualifications such as BTECs, because I believe the latter do a better job of articulating the transferable Skills being developed. And the key point I want to get across here is that all learners are developing transferable Skills through their school and college curriculum learning, not just those learners on vocationally aligned qualifications. I have turned this analysis into the SkillsMap®, which you can also find on the website developed alongside this book. On the website, the SkillsMap allows you to look at the Skills and subjects from a range of different angles, and you can use that tool with your learners too. You can use the SkillsMap as you read through this section if you want to see more examples, but you do not need to in order to understand this section.

In my analysis, I identified and extracted every transferable Skill from each of the curriculums to create a comprehensive database that maps, into categories and sub-categories, all the different Skills that are in the different subject curriculums. At the very top level, there are four categories of transferable Skills that learners develop in pre-18 study, across all academic subjects.

Figure 21. The four categories of transferable Skills

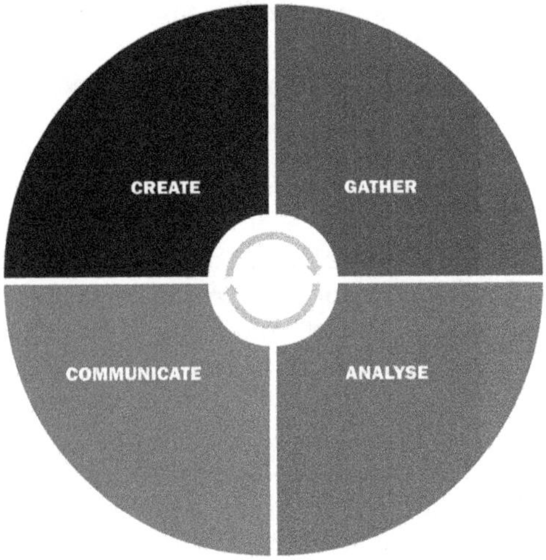

Graphic by Kalina Zlatkova. Summarised from SkillsMap® © Kate Daubney 2020.

And if we look at the sub-categories of transferable Skills that emerge in each of those categories, we start to get a sense of the huge richness of language and definitions available to learners (see Figure 22). Each of these sub-categories then breaks down again, so, for example, *Work with evidence* includes:

- Understand nature of evidence
- Evaluate significance of evidence
- Make connections
- Draw comparisons.

Overall, I have identified more than 200 different transferable Skills that surface from across the different academic curriculums. That is an extraordinary

Figure 22. The sub-categories of transferable Skills

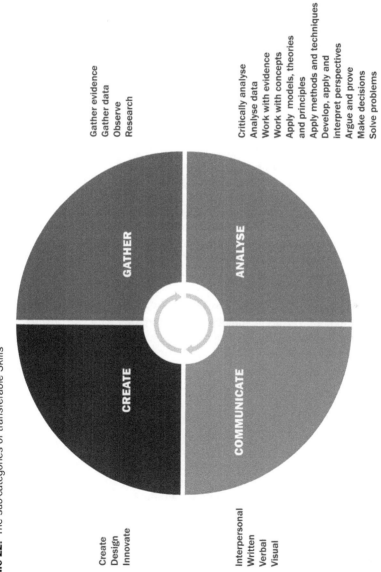

Gather evidence
Gather data
Observe
Research

Critically analyse
Analyse data
Work with evidence
Work with concepts
Apply models, theories and principles
Apply methods and techniques
Develop, apply and interpret perspectives
Argue and prove
Make decisions
Solve problems

GATHER

ANALYSE

CREATE

COMMUNICATE

Create
Design
Innovate

Interpersonal
Written
Verbal
Visual

Graphic by Kalina Zlatkova. Summarised from SkillsMap® © Kate Daubney 2020.

number of different Skills that are often interconnected but clearly distinct from each other.

These 200+ Skills are the Skills that employers want and use. Every role has a combination of these Skills. From *Formulate arguments* to *Evaluate risks*, from *Visual identification* to *Create new approaches to improving perform-ance*, this is the language of study and of work. So, let us make it as easy as possible for learners to become fluent in that language.

Working with such richness does of course have its downsides. I know from working with academics and teachers that when they encounter a list with that level of detail for the first time, they are often completely overwhelmed. '200 Skills?! [*Head falls into hands*]' They know their academic subjects well and have a reasonable sense of the scope of other subjects, and instinctively recognise the picture painted of their own curriculum in Skills terms. But seeing the whole picture is as surprising and breath-taking as it is when you reach the top of a mountain or a tall building and see a familiar landscape from a new perspective for the first time.

So, imagine being a learner and seeing 200 different Skills for the first time. How would that make you feel?

What *can* we do to make that less overwhelming for learners, but still help them get the benefit? And how can we enable learners not only to engage with the richness of language but also help them identify what they are developing through their subject study, at any level?

I think there are four main opportunities for learners to do the following:

1 Understand my subject better – what are the Skills I am developing?
2 Understand how different subjects cluster together – if I like developing and using my creative Skills, for example, what are the other subjects where I can also do that?
3 Understand commonalities across very different subjects – where else do individual Skills or sub-categories of Skills surface?
4 Understand complementarity – how do subjects combine to offer a wider range of different Skills in combination?

Opportunities 2 and 3 offer different angles on the same information: 2 is about providing more detail around subject relationships that learners already have some understanding of; 3 is about opening their eyes to some unexpected con-nections and what that can help them understand about themselves and their future options. Opportunity 4 is about recognising that diversity in subject com-binations is not to be feared and, indeed, is highly developmental in terms of preparing for the transition to work.

So, let's explore.

I want to understand my subject better

There are two Skills sub-categories which turn up in every academic subject, and they are not that surprising: *Critically analyse* and *Written/verbal/visual communication*. Every learner learns to take their subject to pieces to figure out how it all fits together, and every learner has to express what they learn from doing so. But I have identified over thirty different types of critical analysis Skills, so where do we start when introducing learners to these Skills?

Firstly, it is a question of simply **pointing them out**. As I have discussed earlier in this book, our focus on Knowledge gain often overtakes other elements of learning gain, and if you have read the curriculum documents yourself, you will know how much emphasis they place on Knowledge.

So, when a learner is *Making connections* or *Interpreting results*, even saying 'You are using and developing the Skills of *Making connections*' is something a learner may not have heard before. As teachers – and I include myself in this – we do not always do as much as we can to articulate that aspect of the learning experience, so it is no wonder that learners are not aware.

For example, we talk about *Problem-solving* all the time across a huge range of subjects. But how often do we talk about the different phases of solving a problem, or emphasise that there are different approaches to solving the same problem? Thus, instead of only saying, 'There are two ways to solve a quadratic equation', we can also show them the approaches and then build on that by helping learners identify when to take those different approaches to solving the same problem: that would be *Weigh available options*. Which phase of problem-solving are they in at a given stage in the problem? That would be *Understand the concept of problem-solving*. Then we can help them recognise that finding different approaches is a good Skill in its own right.

This type of approach is particularly helpful when learners are doing formative and summative assessments. It can be a great way of supplementing positive feedback:

> 'I really liked the way you presented points of view that are different from those of the author.'

It can also be a way of enabling learners to get more out of the Knowledge they already have:

> 'What other techniques could you have applied to the evidence to deduce something different?'

Secondly, particularly with post-16 learners, I think it is reasonable and manageable to **share categories of Skills** with them. At 16 they are beginning their journey into work and if they are likely to stay in study for two or more years, then the more exposure they have to the language of Skills, the better. It is, after all, the same language.

There are a number of subjects where the transferable Skills are fundamental to the specialist Skills. For example, in the study of Ancient Languages, students learn to research, often for the first time. Helping them to engage with the entire set of Skills required to research effectively means that they quickly grasp the process of researching, as well as being able to see their own progress through that process. They can identify where difficulties lie but also start to see connections between Skills in the same category within their subject, and across to other subjects. Interestingly, nowhere in the curriculum documentation is there an explanation of what research Skills are. It is entirely assumed that learners will know – will have had it explained to them? – what it means to research, and how complex and composite the Skills of research are.

The Skills I identified in the *Research* sub-category of the SkillsMap® include:

• Gather relevant information
• Generate and explore lines of enquiry
• Explore the potential in different opportunities
• Organise information and research findings appropriately.

But *Exploring lines of enquiry* also emerges in creative subjects and in Chemistry. *Exploring the potential in different opportunities* surfaces in Physical Education as well as Media Studies and Business Studies. Learners are already learning to see their subjects from different points of view. So, why not see the Skills of those subjects from different points of view too?

I want to understand how different subjects cluster together

I made the point in the Knowledge section of the book that learners are often strongly encouraged to think about academic alignment of subjects. Beyond foundational Knowledge relationships – Maths as a foundation for Physics – these interconnections between subjects rarely cross disciplinary Knowledge areas. Thus, science subjects are grouped together, as are creative practice or more traditional humanities. Even in preparing my Skills analysis, I found myself drifting into some assumptions about where subjects grouped or fitted together, and had to reflect deliberately on how to avoid that in order to be impartial about the subjects and their Skills. Working in an educational institution where organisational structures reinforce those groupings means it can often be really challenging to find another way to look at that clustering.

I mentioned earlier that one of the impacts of the pandemic has been to accelerate some aspects of the digital, virtual, and automated Fourth Industrial Revolution. With such an emphasis on technology, and our creative sectors so damaged economically, arts and humanities disciplines continue to suffer, building on the policy climate that has promoted STEM as a universal panacea or solution to change. But my approach to surfacing and articulating the huge range of transferable Skills within these subject areas enables us to realise quickly that these disciplines offer many of the same transferable Skills as the STEM subjects. For example, it will not be a surprise to any student of humanities subjects that *Develop, apply, and interpret perspectives* is a Skill category common to History, Philosophy, English Literature, and Classical Civilisation, among others. But it is also common to Economics, Politics, and Law. And to Dance, Drama, and Music. And to Design and Technology, Electronics, and

Music Technology. And to Environmental Science, Geology, and Computer Science. As a category of Skills, its reach is enormous and in depth across social sciences, humanities and arts, sciences and technology.

Subjects do cluster together very strongly around different Skill categories, and some of the subjects that are perceived to be traditional humanities have incredible coverage in depth of the Skills in the Analyse category and the Communications category. This will feel like a safe Skills space to learners who were perhaps put off pre-16 by subjects where they were not able to master some of the Skills that lie more commonly outside humanities subjects, such as *Applying methods and techniques* or *Solving problems*. If they found those Skills challenging to master in Chemistry or Maths, and found it easier in English and History to *Develop perspectives*, it is no surprise that they may want to stay on safe ground Skills-wise. It is really important to enable learners to recognise that. An apparent narrowness in Skills development is perhaps inevitable if learners stick to a very tight disciplinary combination. But that recognition is also a cornerstone in coming to terms with Skills gain more holistically, and it can help learners feel less disconnected from other subjects if they can recognise also where commonalities in Skills emerge.

Furthermore, if we look at breadth as well as depth, the surfacing of both *Critically analyse* and communication in *Written/verbal/visual* in every subject can be quite freeing. And imagine an A Level choice event in your school or college where subjects were presented by Skill clusters and not by subjects or disciplines or organisational departments. Quite often students of science would not think of themselves as using those two Skills groups, but they are just as fundamental as they are in English Literature or Philosophy. And if we go for a less commonly developed Skill sub-category like *Innovate*, we can start to unpick our assumptions about subject relationships. And, by extension, our assumptions about the types of learners who might study subject combinations. That latter is incredibly important as part of effective Career decision-making, because it gets learners out of the disciplinary pigeonholes and perceived linearity or lack of aligned Careers choices, and moves them towards thinking about themselves and what interests them in and of itself.

Now I mentioned earlier that learners (and teachers) can be really overwhelmed by choice. Nowhere is this more true than in the **Paralysis Challenge** I identified at the start of the book. For example, if we start with 35 post-16 A Level subjects, for example, and then suggest a learner picks any three of them, in theory they have over 6,500 combinations! Academic alignment and the disciplinary clustering form a way of ruling some of those out, not to mention timetabling logistics of course. And all of these have provided justifications for how learners have historically been supported to narrow down their subject choices from 6,500 to one or two.

If we look at History, Politics, and Film Studies, for example, we can see commonalities in the application and development of Skills to *Work with concepts, Develop, apply, and interpret perspectives*, and *Interpersonal communication*. These seem obvious to us, and learners studying subjects with commonalities like this will experience significant synergies in their learning, as well as nuances in how those are applied in different subject contexts. That is a good thing, of course.

But when we start to look in more depth at Skill relationships and start with the Skills synergies across all subjects, we open up commonalities and connections that put far more subject combinations and choices back on the table. And actually these are good, conscious choices that reflect the learner's own values. We all know learners who have a weaker subject, one they enjoy less than the others. What if they could find a subject that did not obviously fit with the others, but actually played to more of their Skills strengths? We also know learners who have a yearning to take a subject that does not appear to fit with the others but there does not seem to be an obvious justification for taking it. Again, looking at the Skills involved in those subjects and looking for commonalities reveal why combinations that look quirky or unrealistic might actually play very much to an individual learner's strengths.

Let us take these four subjects as an example:

- Business Studies
- Design and Technology
- Electronics
- Environmental Science.

What do they have in common? Well, 'not humanities' seems to be obvious, and in some schools or colleges, some of these subjects might be considered 'less academic'. But all four of them also strongly feature Skills that belong to *Innovate*, as well as those belonging to *Analyse data, Apply models, theories, and principles*, and *Solve problems*.

Let's look at another three subjects:

- Dance
- Geology
- Sociology.

Again, a quirky combination at first sight, but they all require Skills to *Apply methods and techniques, Research*, and to *Develop, apply, and interpret perspectives*. For an analytically minded student, there is a lot of common ground here. Likewise, Drama, Physics, and Geology, the example I used earlier in this section, feature significant commonality in Skills from the Observe category.

I am not advocating what would be seen by many as complete intellectual and cross-disciplinary anarchy (not to mention becoming the villain for all colleagues tasked with timetabling in schools and colleges!). But I am advocating for a different approach to be taken to how we talk to learners about how they experience the subjects they enjoy. There are very good reasons why these commonalities surface in what look like superficially dysfunctional combinations. And let us not undermine the learners who see that before we do, but cannot explain it for themselves and are not getting a satisfactory answer out of us either. Let us dig down into why those connections exist, help learners understand how their instinctive enjoyment of subjects is surfacing in this way, and how to make good decisions as a consequence. A learner who can articulate that to themselves and to an employer makes a strong case for the intellectual value of diversity.

I want to understand commonalities across very different subjects

Another opportunity for learners emerges when we start to dig down even deeper into those connections. We see some fascinating links that really support students to pivot through their learning experiences and focus on how individual Skills underpin their subject learning in different ways. Until the time when government fundamentally rewrites its approach to curriculum statements and enables teachers to fully realise the Skills value of academic curriculum (hopefully drawing on some of the thinking in this book!), this is going to be beyond the scope of day-to-day delivery for almost everyone. But if you are considering any kind of cross-school projects or collaborations, or want to do some creative activities to support learners as they start their subject decision-making, this is something to consider.

Let us look at a couple of examples. One of my favourite Skills (because I do it all the time!) is *Make connections*, which is in the Skills used to *Critically analyse*. Now *Critically analyse* is the sub-category that turns up in every subject, but not all the Skills appear in every subject. *Make connections* is developed in:

- Economics
- Philosophy
- Physical Education.

What can we do with that? Well, we could *Make connections* between the subjects, for a start. Classical philosophers like Plato were very interested in the role of physical activity in moral development of the human condition, but classical philosophy is full of connectedness as philosophers sought to make sense of their environment and those who live in it.

Physical Education and sport generally are now well understood as part of the fabric of our society, and fundamental to identity in many key respects. Sports increasingly rely on connections between biomechanics, nutrition, textiles, and product design to maximise performance. And behind all those aspects, as well as identity, is the economics of it: think of the brand of a football team like Liverpool or a baseball team like the New York Yankees. Then think about how interwoven personal identity and visual brand are, and the economic reliance of those sporting organisations on their brand and how people buy literally into it, even when they do not follow the sport. Many people go to New York and buy a New York Yankees baseball cap, without any idea what the NY logo actually represents. From there we can close the circle by thinking about game theory and decision theory, both key to Philosophy and to Economics – and, of course, to sport.

That is a rather expansive example, but as a cross-year or cross-school project it offers a huge amount of potential to explore subjects and ideas, and also to develop endlessly and in many different directions how learners *Make connections*. Some teaching in higher education has now taken on this more holistic approach, bringing students from different and diverse subjects together to focus on projects or problem-solving, and it is very much the way that businesses work, creating teams with diverse roles and functions to take projects through a complete lifecycle.

A different example would be *Make and record observations*. The Skills categorised under *Observe* cover subjects as diverse as Classical Civilisation, Physics, Film Studies, and Computer Science. Bringing artistic students to look at code or physics phenomena introduces them to different ways to use their observation Skills. Film Studies students, practised at analysing visual framing and unpacking narratives, can look differently at archaeological evidence and classical artefacts. Asking learners to share what *they* see when they observe the raw material of another subject is beneficial for learners of both subjects.

There is much to be gained by bringing learners of different subjects together to reflect on what it is like to study each other's subjects. Learners can sometimes feel quite defensive about their choices post-16, due to the **Challenges** around **Paralysis** and the **Hourglass**. So, seeing their subject through other eyes and explaining it to others, including in terms of Skills developed, can help them take ownership of what they enjoy about it. It will also really help prepare for the transition to work, when they will be repeatedly asked to transfer Skills through different situations, and when they are asked to or need to learn new Skills.

As soon as you find commonality, new demands seem less daunting. And that will be fundamental as artificial intelligence and economic change have an increasing impact on the employment market. It is not simply about the need for human creative Skills in shaping artificial intelligence, but about something far more essential in enabling individuals to continue to adapt to a changing employment landscape. The vulnerability of blue-collar roles to automation can imply that once these roles become obsolete, those who had those roles cease to be able to make a contribution in work. But all roles require transferable Skills in different combinations, and the key to transition into new roles is finding commonalities to enable pivot and refocus. An experienced lorry driver has much to teach programmers of automated vehicles about how human beings make decisions both behind the wheel and around other vehicles, which will be essential during the transition from solely human drivers to any future full automation, such as in negotiating urban areas with pedestrians. That requires analysis, looking for patterns, breaking down problems, and evaluating risk. Those Skills will find their combination in new roles that emerge, and provide a platform too for upskilling through adult education. Again, that requires a policy shift, but it is not insurmountable with a proper infrastructure for how we talk about Skills in curriculum.

I want to understand complementarity

Finally, let us acknowledge the importance of difference and contrast. Some learners like to be stretched in different ways. They do not seek synergy, but contrast and stretch. They like the 'head swap' that occurs when they move between subjects. They like the fact that they see the world differently, and all the intellectual and personal challenges that come with that.

Analysis of subject-transferable Skills might reveal that the differences are not as stark as first perceived: I gave some examples in the previous sections that showed what might be seen as untraditional subject combinations. But for all their commonalities, Dance, Physics, and English Language is a bit of an unusual combination, and learners, parents, carers, and teachers might be nervous about how to explain that on a university application form or a job application. So, how can we support learners to be at ease with that and, almost as importantly, put others at ease?

I've mentioned before that one of the greatest **Challenges** is narrowing definitions of success, and when combined with the **Hourglass Phenomenon**, learners can feel very much that their voice in their choice is the least important element. I strongly believe – and have years of working with learners to evidence this – that the better job we do in building learners' confidence to take ownership of what they like and how they talk about it, the better they will be able to make effective Careers decisions, whatever landscape they find themselves in. Thus, a learner who can talk with confidence about how they see the balance of the improvised creativity of Dance with the logical application of theories in Physics with the understanding of the concept of significance in English Language, is also a learner who can talk about the importance of recognising patterns in all three subjects. And when we think about how many Career choices those Skills alone open up, we know we have laid the foundations for an able future employee, freelancer, or entrepreneur.

And while we are on the topic of the unfashionable, I want to take a moment to acknowledge what are often seen as the least academic of subjects, and – I am sad to say – the subjects that are often associated with less academically confident or competent learners. Those of us who advocate for the importance of learner choice, whatever it is, often find ourselves standing against a tidal wave of perception about apparently strong and weak subjects. So, I was delighted to identify in my analysis how many of those often perceived as unfashionable, 'unacademic' subjects had the greatest diversity of transferable Skills. Given the 19 sub-categories of transferable Skills in my SkillsMap®, the following had 11 or more different sub-categories developed through their curriculum. In descending order (the most sub-categories first), they are:

- Design and Technology
- Environmental Science
- Geography
- Physical Education
- Sociology

- Geology
- Computer Science
- Electronics
- English Language
- Music Technology
- Drama
- Media Studies
- Psychology
- Archaeology
- Business Studies
- Dance
- Film Studies
- History of Art.

These subjects rank so highly in Skills development because they draw on more than principally the *Analyse* and *Communicate* categories. So, imagine what will a learner of even one of these subjects, let alone two or more, bring to the workplace? They will bring a huge range of transferable Skills already in development across all four of the top level Skills categories in the graphic earlier. That learner is ready to become an employee with huge potential across a range of roles, and has lots of different reference points for starting a wide range of Careers journeys.

This also provides a strong argument in favour of suggesting students balance more traditional academic subjects that might have a narrower but deeper range of Skill categories (Physics, History) with newer ones that have far greater scope of Skills (Design and Technology, Sociology). But if we are to enable learners to do so with confidence, educators and policy-makers and parents/carers will need to abandon the perception of 'strong' traditional subjects and 'weak' new subjects. Because if you are thinking about preparing learners for work, particularly in a fluid and unpredictable economic landscape, then strengthening their platform and maximising their starting position have got to be the priority. Therefore, we might argue in Skills terms for a more structured approach to helping learners combine 'specialised' traditional subjects and 'broad' new subjects with each other.

So, what does this new perspective on Skills offer your community of teachers and Careers educators? Here are some suggestions.

Activities if you and your teaching colleagues have minimal time to do anything new

- Introduce Employability by introducing learners to the language of Skills
  - Use the Skills graphics in this section to introduce learners to the idea that these Skills are not separate from their studies or added on, but are already being developed through their studies

- Using an individual sub-category of Skills, such as *Solve problems* or *Make decisions*, encourages learners to share examples of when they solve problems or make decisions in their classroom learning or home-work in different subjects
- Build connections in how you talk about Skills in relation to subject study and Careers
  - Connect academic Skill sub-categories to the same Skills you talk about in different roles and Careers, helping learners see the connections between apparently different areas like Dance and airplane pilot (*Make Decisions*) or Physics and advertising executive (*Apply models, theories, and principles*)
  - Twenty Questions: In small groups, ask learners to think about either roles or subjects using the same lists of Skills, then describe the role or subject only in terms of the Skills used. How much information can be drawn out about transferable Skills before the specialist Skills or Knowledge of the subject or role are revealed?
- Review the way in which subjects are presented as a post-16 choice to learners
  - Bring post-16 learners in to talk to pre-16 learners about their subjects, and structure conversations so they can identify and talk about the Skills they are developing; then engage your pre-16 learners to build the con-nections between those subjects
  - Engage learners in discussions about the experience of making post-16 subject choices. Where do they feel pressure? When are decisions easy or difficult? How do they see the relationships between subjects? What hap-pens to how those decisions feel when they move away from Knowledge similarities towards Skills similarities? What information would they find helpful that they do not feel they can currently access?
  - Introduce Skills as a way of thinking about how subjects relate to each other and how commonalities are defined in different ways.

Additional activities for you if you want to start looking at Skills differently and have time and capacity to do so

- Work through curriculum documentation with teaching colleagues to iden-tify which Skills surface in each of their subjects, and embed that under-standing in how the subject is taught and discussed, both with learners and with teaching colleagues
  - Encourage teaching colleagues to articulate the Skills in use to learners
- Find ways to share the Skills in each subject visibly through different kinds of learning space and content
  - Learners' familiarity will increase enormously if they keep seeing and hearing about the Skills they use and develop
- In Careers activities, use the same Skills language when you talk to learners about their study interests and challenges

- o Introducing Skills (and Attributes) helps learners understand why they enjoy different subjects or find them challenging
- o This will help learners develop a more nuanced understanding of themselves, which underpins effective decision-making
- Dig deeper into the Skills relationships between subjects
  - o What are the commonalities between subjects that we have otherwise seen as very different?
- Gather colleagues together from different subject areas and disciplines using Skills commonalities
  - o Encourage discussion and sharing of how the same Skills are developed differently in different subjects
  - o Enable teaching colleagues to see more of how their subjects connect at the level of transferable Skills
  - o Encourage teaching colleagues to present discussions about this to learners in assemblies or online learning
- Bring learners of different subjects together to reflect on each other's subject choices
- Enable them to take ownership of what they enjoy about their subjects by seeing them through other learners' eyes and vice versa.

All of these Activities can be supported by using the material on the SkillsMap® website developed alongside this book.

Messages for learners

My qualifications are not just about gaining Knowledge, but also help me develop a wide range of different transferable and specialist Skills

I can recognise transferable Skills when I use them in my academic study and in my other activities

I am constantly developing new transferable Skills in my academic study and in my other activities

I understand how I use the same transferable Skills in different subjects, in both similar and different ways

My diverse interests across subjects are a reflection of what interests me, and where my Skills abilities and interests lie

Diversity of interests and Skills is really valuable when I am choosing my next step, making Career decisions, or changing direction

If I find my first choice of favourite subjects seems a bit strange or random to other people, I can look more deeply at what Skills the subjects have in common to help me feel more comfortable with my choices and explain them better to others

Seeing how Skills I use are also used in other subjects can help me see my own subjects differently

Skills are the threads that connect everything I study and do in my working life; they get thicker and thinner along the way, depending on how much I use them, but they are always there and I will always learn new Skills.

Notes

1 As an educator and researcher, I am fully supportive of the view that education for education's sake is a good thing and nothing in this section is intended to undermine that. But the reality is that education is increasingly a focus in society, policy, and government as the runway to employment, and in my opinion it is better to face that head on.

2 This is not a scholarly theoretical book, but a practical one, so I have not elaborated further here on how learners actually develop their Skills. But if you are interested in the pedagogy, I find DeKeyser's Skill Acquisition Theory a useful concept. DeKeyser identifies a stage called 'declarative knowledge' (e.g. There is a Skill called 'making connections'), followed by 'procedural knowledge' (e.g. This is what it means to 'make connections' and this is how 'make connections' is applied alongside Skills of 'evaluate the significance of key factors' and 'sift arguments') (p. 95). His final stage, the 'Automatization of knowledge' of those Skills (p. 96), is the aspiration for successful learners in the workplace, but I would propose that 'procedural knowledge' is the most important stage for learners to make an effective preparation for and transition into work. This is because the level of self-awareness is not only desired by employers, but also what they need to make connections between study and their choice of Career or first workplace role. See DeKeyser, R. (2015) 'Skill acquisition theory', in VanPatten, B. and Williams, J. (eds) *Theories in Second Language Acquisition: An Introduction*, 2nd edition. London: Routledge, pp. 94–112.

3 My A levels were in Maths, Physics, and Music, and my undergraduate degree is in Maths and Music. No one ever tires of telling me that Maths and Music go well together.

4 All content presented in this book from the SkillsMap® is © Kate Daubney 2020. You can find out more about SkillsMap® by visiting yourskillsmap.com.

5 As of February 2020, this initial A Level research has been fully cross-referenced with Scottish qualifications and GCSEs. Given that definitions of curriculum in relation to subject discipline tend to be fairly consistent, the findings of my A Level research can reasonably be taken to be representative of other similar subject curriculums taught in the UK and internationally in terms of their Skill base. The findings are also consonant with my pre-existing research on UK higher education curriculum; the Skills surfaced at pre-18 are more limited in number, detail, and scope. You can read more about my research in Appendix 5.

Experience

For school and college leavers, Experience means something different to what it means at and after university. During higher education, for a range of reasons, students have access to a more diverse range of work experiences. Those might include specific Career-related internships, as well as subsistence roles to earn money such as bar work, retail, health care, or administrative roles. As **Careers Activity 7: Make Experience Meaningful** describes, Experiences of all types, lengths, and relevance to work are fundamental to making good Careers decisions. This is the key area where Employability and Careers overlap with each other. When learners reflect effectively on why they did or did not enjoy something, and what the Experience was made up of, their response is really helpful in exploring and defining future choices. That applies both academically and in Careers decisions.

As I have noted before, Experience at all levels of education is also gained through activities outside education: hobbies, interests, enterprise projects, volunteering, family caring responsibilities, and other activities. This is quite often the sort of Experience that pre-18 learners draw on when thinking about or trying to demonstrate their suitability for work, because they can more readily see how they are already using and developing different Attributes and Skills. Sports teams, business clubs, theatre groups, music groups, and hobby clubs, for example, offer a wide range of Experiences that require Attributes like patience, determination, commitment, and enthusiasm, as well as many of the *Interpersonal* Communication Skills required for working with others. Likewise, caring for a family member requires Skills of organisation, attention to detail, gathering information, and relationships, as well as many Attributes related to empathy, self-management, and resilience.

But what is far less well understood, or exploited to the benefit of learners, is that Experience is also gained through academic study. The application of Knowledge, Attributes, and Skills to the activities of learning and the processes of assessment are important sources of Experience for learners to benefit from. Those Experiences develop self-awareness and offer an opportunity to explore how Attributes and Skills are applied. The Experience of seeing an eighteenth-century manuscript of music or literature or historical account, of thinking about the person who wrote it, what they were trying to share, of imagining, evaluating, deciding, researching: these are all ways in which Experience in academic curriculum surfaces the Attributes and Skills. Likewise, dissecting your first worm is about exploring your tolerance for the unknown, following instructions, observing and describing, precision and attention to detail. Shaping a piece of clay, testing the tolerance of the material for weight, shape, stretching, bending, water, and touch, all stimulate curiosity, inspiration, humour, investigation, and analysis. Walking around a city, looking at how canals, railways, and roads intersect is applying the Knowledge of how built communities evolve and using observation Skills to begin to experience the differences in architecture and urban designs.

A huge amount of benefit can be realised by helping learners identify that they are not just acquiring Knowledge, but experiencing the application of Knowledge, and the development of their Attributes and Skills both now and with future consequences. Many years ago, I tutored a Maths GCSE learner, who could not get her head around quadratic equations. Unlike percentages or some of the other numerical maths where you might be able to easily conjure up a real-world situation to keep learning momentum going when things got tough, my mind went blank when she slammed down her pen, the chair flew back, and the door slammed behind her as she left. 'What's the (…) point of quadratic equations?' she yelled from another room. And while all the academic future uses of quadratic equations came quickly to my mind, in that moment I could not think of another non-academic purpose.

So, what was the learner's Experience in that situation? Well, it was partly about Attributes like persistence and sticking at something when it is difficult. We might even argue that it is also about the ability to still do something even when you are not sure why it is important: that comes up in working life more often than we might like, and it is the direct opposite of encouraging learners to think and act independently, of course. But it is also about improving through practice, about moving pieces of learning and understanding around so you can see them from different points of view. It is about learning to think in non-linear ways that stretch our brains. It is about the Experience of challenge and difficulty. It is about the practical application of the Knowledge Maths provides about the processes of breaking something into pieces to make it easier to deal with, and trying other ways to look at something in order to progress the solution. That is what we Experience every time we do something new in so many academic subjects. Yet we do not do enough to enable or encourage learners to see their learning in this way. If we did more, when an employer asks a learner, 'Tell me about something you had to do that was really hard', the learner can say, 'Let me tell you what I learned from hating quadratic equations.'

I think that can help to connect these two perspectives together: Experience in non-academic and academic contexts. When learners think about their Experiences within the academic context, the same approach applies as it does non-academically. 'That was more fun than I thought it was going to be' applies equally to scaling your first climbing wall or playing in a band as it does to dissecting your first worm or seeing lithium react with water. So, enabling teaching colleagues to help learners reflect on their Experiences through curriculum is a good way to start bridging the gap between the academic and non-academic Experiences that learners have.

It is also useful to reflect on the pandemic and its impact on gaining Experience, again in both academic and non-academic contexts. Most, if not all of your learners are likely to have missed out on workplace visits, work shadowing, or work experience weeks unless you were able to identify employers who offered something virtually. But it is incredibly important to help learners identify that the transition to online learning and the personal changes individuals made during the pandemic are of interest to employers. While Careers Leaders, Careers professionals, and teachers will have gone out of their way to make the transition as easy as possible to online learning, there is value in shining a light on that transition. I will explore later the differences between the digital Skills that learners have in their personal space and those of the workplace, but in practice the digital Skills of online learning in school and college will be relatively similar to those in the workplace: independent discovery, task management, concentrating in synchronous delivery or meetings, and so on. Likewise, employers have been asking higher education students and graduates, 'What did you do differently in the first lockdown? What did you learn, what did you try, how did you approach things creatively or innovatively? Who did you help?' There is an expectation that post-18 learners will have been opportunity-facing in the crisis. Again, I will discuss that more later, but it is all part of a wider reflective process for learners on what their Experiences are, and how they see them.

Activities for you

- Introduce Employability by talking about Experience
  - Experiences are personal and belong to the individual
  - Experiences are really helpful also for thinking about Career choices: why do I like doing that thing? (academic or non-academic)
  - Learners are constantly having different academic and non-academic Experiences: identify what those are in a typical week
- Scenario discussions for different roles
  - Which Experiences would be useful if you were doing this role for the first time?
    - If you were going up in a rocket or climbing down into a sewer for the first time, what learning experiences have you had that might help you imagine what that is like?
    - Building on that, being a plumber or a rocket scientist or a jeweller or an app designer is very often about solving problems: what other times have you had to solve problems?
  - What examples can the learner give of a time when they had a similar Experience, either in their learning or outside school/college?
- Create some learning gains with teaching colleagues before field trips or new classroom activities, so learners go into an Experience with an idea of how to identify the Knowledge, Attributes, and Skills that are applied or used during the Experience
  - Articulate to learners before an academic Experience what to look out for

- o Enable learners to reflect on what they learned about the Experience in terms of applying Knowledge, drawing on Attributes, or applying specialist and transferable Skills
- o Enable learners to reflect on what they learned about themselves in terms of applying Knowledge, drawing on Attributes, or applying specialist and transferable Skills
- All Experiences are useful for learning: from playing in a concert to an apprenticeship open day to voluntary work with a wildlife trust or visiting an old people's home. Learners take responsibility for realising the benefit of Experiences by being self-aware of them.

Messages for learners

Experiences help me decide what I like and don't like and what's important in my future choices

Experiences outside school and college help me demonstrate what employers are looking for

Experiences through my academic study give me lots of ways to demonstrate the Attributes and Skills that employers are looking for

When I talk about my Experiences inside and outside school/college, it is helpful to have some examples

– What evidence do I have that I enjoyed this Experience of building an electrical circuit/designing a clock/reading this novel?

– How can I describe what different Experiences were like, in terms of the Attributes I drew on or Skills I used?

I know what changed for me when I had a particular academic or non-academic Experience: I loved it/hated it/didn't understand it then but do understand it now.

In Around Beyond[1]

Hopefully, you now have a clear understanding of what Employability is, how it is innate to the academic curriculum that learners get taught in schools, colleges, and higher education, and how to surface all its elements with learners so they can capture the benefit more quickly and carry it forward. In this section, I am going to explore the relationship between Employability and academic subject choices that helps learners see how their curriculum learning connects to Careers, not just in STEM subjects but in every subject they might choose.

As mentioned previously, Benchmark 4: Linking Curriculum Learning to Careers creates the expectation of learners seeing and acting on the relationship between their subject choices and their future Career options. In the examples offered for this connection that relate to STEM, there is a strong linear connection implied. While it is logical in some ways, in others, I think it creates a very strong culture of exclusion. What about learners who are not interested in STEM subjects? Does that mean their curriculum learning does not link to future careers or societal value? As we all contribute to the recovery of our global economic and professional ecosystem in the wake of the pandemic, it would be completely wrong to suggest that we only need people with a STEM focus. And what about learners who are not studying STEM subjects but might be interested in working in STEM sectors? Technology companies often complain that they cannot access sufficient post-18 learners or graduates from the 'right' technical subjects. But if they changed the way they recruited to bring in a wider diversity of learners and graduates from different subjects with a wider range of transferable Skills, those recruits could learn the specialist Skills those recruiters want from inside the technology company. It just requires a change of strategy and a change of perspective. Furthermore, from a social mobility and social justice point of view, that linear connection is simply not justifiable, and it is also poor education both academically and in the Careers sense.

The problem though is far greater than STEM, and again it reflects **Challenge 2**, which is that if qualifications are positioned as Knowledge assets, learners (both young and adult) find it very difficult to make what look like non-linear connections between academic subjects and Careers choices. This might seem an elaborate way to make the point, but why shouldn't an adult learner do a History A Level as part of reskilling to become a tax auditor? Maths or Accountancy might seem more literally useful but, as I have demonstrated in the Skills section, History not only provides a way of developing very relevant Skills to the specialism of tax audit, but would also develop a portfolio of communication Skills that also enables the learner to be good at working with clients and colleagues, in a way that a Maths A Level might not.

So, a model that helps learners map and explain the connections between academic choices and Career choices – and how Employability assets forge those connections – creates a strong link between Careers and Employability, and enables learners to make better-informed choices academically. For while the SkillsMap® is in itself a key part of connecting academic and Career choices, sometimes learners want to look at the bigger picture before they get stuck into the detail.

A model that achieved this would also address **Challenge 1: The Hourglass Phenomenon** by keeping more options on the table for longer so that learners could see ahead beyond the next step. It would also address **Challenge 3: Paralysis** by making it easier to see how choices are grouped together, and enabling the learner to focus on which type of choice appeals most to them.

Such a model is not complicated, and you could think of it most simply as being a matter of the proximity of a Career choice to an academic subject (see Figure 23). Let us take one A Level subject as an example: Mathematics and Statistics.

Careers IN Mathematics and Statistics are those that use the subject Knowledge directly. Some examples would include:[2]

Figure 23. In Around Beyond

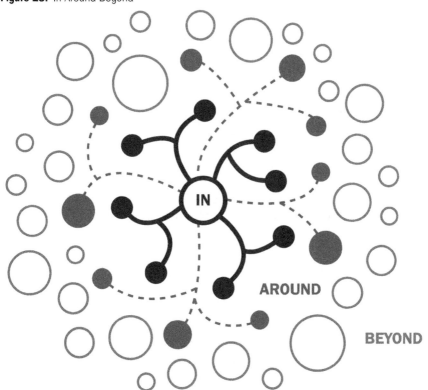

- Football Statistician analysing on-field performance to inform strategy
- Actuary modelling lifespans to assess risk in pension plans
- Passenger Analyst for public transport or airlines, modelling flow and usage to support safety, security, and transportation scheduling
- Accountant
- Investment Analyst in a bank.

Careers AROUND Maths still use something derived from Mathematics or Statistics as a subject, but more indirectly applied, such as:

- Meteorologist
- Seismologist
- Quantity surveyor
- Software developer
- Insurance underwriter.

Careers BEYOND Maths… well, this is where it gets difficult and Benchmark 4 creates issues, because … well … Anything is possible! Literally! It is a well-worn phrase by now, but Maths students and graduates are highly employable. But how to choose? That is surely creating **Paralysis by Possibilities**. But I promised you that In Around Beyond would solve the Paralysis problems.

So what do we really mean by BEYOND? Let's try again with History.

Careers IN History. There seem to be fewer options here, but they are all still good ones:

- Professional historian (such as Lucy Worsley or Neil Oliver)
- Archivist of historical documents
- Museum curator
- Heritage site manager

Careers AROUND History give us some broad and quite creative choices with clear overlaps with some other academic subjects or wider interests. They might include:

- Diplomat
- Politician
- Costume designer for film or theatre
- Antique valuer or auctioneer

Careers BEYOND History. Well, here we already have an example. Tax Auditor. Let's go back to my explanation earlier. It is simply about spelling out what it is to be a student of a subject, and then do a bit of reverse engineering. For Careers beyond History we are not concerned with the Knowledge, because we do not expect it to be connected to the Career choice. That leaves:

Attributes:

- Persistence
- Objectivity
- Curiosity (among others).

Skills:

- Forensic attention to detail
- Find primary sources of evidence
- Manage and organise large amounts of evidence
- Dig deep into evidence to find the most relevant pieces
- Identify which evidence is important for different arguments or points of view
- Compare and contrast different points of view
- See things from different points of view
- Synthesise a narrative by connecting evidence and information
- Write and present narratives in compelling ways.

So if we looked for other Careers that required this particular combination, we might find:

- Business consultancy
- Solicitor or barrister
- Policy-maker
- Detective
- Journalist
- Environmental activist
- Poverty campaigner ...

... and so on. And then if we added in all the other Attributes and Skills that are innate to being a Historian, we can end up with quite a long list, which can be combined in different ways to align with different Career choices. Now, as I admitted earlier, this can lead to the unintended consequence of **Paralysis by Possibilities**, and I will come back to that shortly. But what thinking like this reveals is a pretty straightforward way of looking at the relationship between Career choices and subject study (see Figure 24).

Hopefully, this model is fairly self-explanatory, but just in case it is not, the key features are:

- Careers IN
  - Emphasise more of the application and further development of the Knowledge and specialist Skills of the subject area; new, related Knowledge will be developed by applying the ability to learn

Figure 24. Applying Knowledge, learning, Attributes, and Skills to In Around Beyond

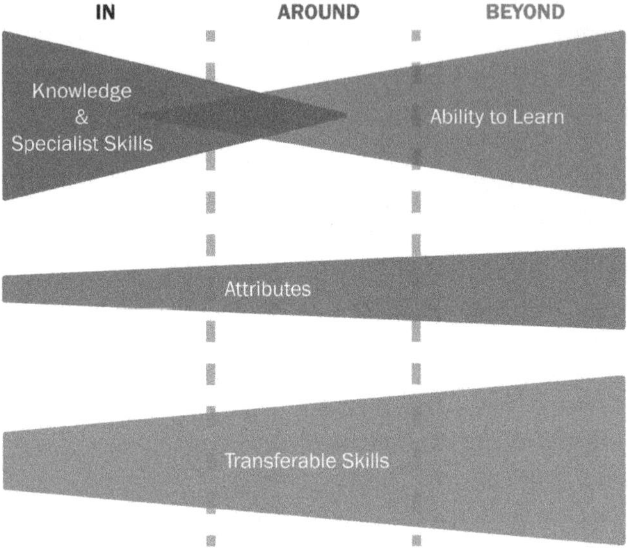

Graphic by Kalina Zlatkova. © Kate Daubney 2021.

- o Require the core Attributes innate to the subject (and others may be developed, depending on the role and sector)
  - o Require the core transferable Skills innate to the subject (and others may be developed, depending on the role and sector)
- Careers AROUND
  - o Begin to de-emphasise the existing Knowledge and specialist Skills of the subject area, and increase emphasis on the ability to learn related and unrelated Knowledge
  - o Require a more diverse range of Attributes than are innate to the subject
  - o Require a more diverse range of transferable Skills than are innate to the subject
- Careers BEYOND
  - o Entirely rely on the ability to learn, and that takes on increasing emphasis the more unconnected the Career is to any subject Knowledge
  - o Require a more diverse range of Attributes, including those related to learning new Knowledge and specialist Skills
  - o Require a more diverse range of transferable Skills, including those related to learning new Knowledge and specialist Skills.

In summary, the more you move towards Careers choices Beyond, the more the ability to learn and develop new Attributes and transferable Skills comes into play. This is why Employability – and understanding what it is, how it is developed, and how to apply it – are so important for learners.

But this is also incredibly useful as a factor in Careers decision-making. Because instead of standing in a huge field of relatively undifferentiated Careers choices and using only the learner's personal interests to guide the choice, learners now have the awareness of their Attributes and transferable Skills – and which ones they want to deploy and develop – to help them draw on. That immediately starts to focus options and choices. They can also reflect on their desire or interest to learn new things and for that learning to become a feature of their future. This relieves some of the Paralysis, because learners have a series of lenses or, if you like, sets in a Venn diagram. As those lenses come into focus, or the sets start to overlap, the choices start to narrow. The difference is that instead of going through the hourglass in an undifferentiated way, narrowing choices and then suddenly exploding them wide open ('I can do anything?!?!'), we enable the learner to see 'I *can* do anything, but I am more likely to enjoy and/or be successful at something that aligns my interests, my Attributes, and my Skills, and might have proximity to my subject interest too.'

And no matter which hourglass they are passing through – secondary, further, or higher education – no matter the mixture of breadth of subjects or depth of study, a self-aware learner who knows what their Attributes and Skills are, and is comfortable with their relative enthusiasm for learning, can explore decisions in relation not just to their interests but also to their subject proximity.

It also explains one of the issues I think can arise with profiling tools. If you ask a learner a series of defining questions about their Attributes, Skills, and interests, but without taking them through a process that either anchors permanently that self-awareness, or connects it to their academic study, you are effectively leading them blind into a series of choices that have no root in their Careers decision-making at a conscious level.

I do not think this is rocket science, in that we have long had the option to direct learners towards qualifications and choices that relate closely to Careers choices through BTECs and now apprenticeships. But I think this way of talking about Employability and linking curriculum learning to Careers gives us the missing link that actually maps for the learner how they make those decisions, and what the components are in those decisions that are not simply a question of Knowledge and relationships to subjects. It also provides that all-important missing link between education and work. It is a link that has always been there, but which education systems are spectacularly poorly constructed at surfacing.

The problem with any choice that seems built on a Knowledge outcome – whether that is Chemistry or Countryside Management – is that at no point have we shown the learner what the other elements are of their transition from education into work. Employability – as captured through Knowledge, Attributes, Skills, Experience, and applied to the In Around Beyond model – gives us connected ways to show learners what that transition looks like. That bridges the gap for them, and employers benefit by recruiting more self-aware employees who understand better what awaits them on their working journey.

And in the longer term, of course, and as we know from our own experience of work, we will always be faced with a next step in our Career that is either close to where we currently are – an In choice in relation to our professional Knowledge – or feels more like a pivot or a leap, or sometimes complete change – an Around or a Beyond choice that draws much more on our accumulated Attributes, Skills, and Experience. So, understanding Employability is not just valuable now. It is fundamental to confident, successful long-term Careers decision-making.

Activities for you

- Use the In Around Beyond model to introduce learners to the way in which Careers and Employability connect to each other
- Map Careers choices you have been discussing with learners against In, Around, or Beyond in relation to specific academic subjects
    - How can you build connections to a Career choice when it doesn't obviously relate to an academic subject?
    - How do people get started on new Career choices when they haven't studied it before?
- Discuss with learners their appetite and interest in exploring what seem unfamiliar areas of Knowledge and Skills
    - Why might this feel exciting or risky?
    - How can that risk be minimised and the excitement of doing something new be made more appealing?
- Comparing jobs In and Around a subject. What are the differences and similarities? For example:
    - Football Statistician and Meteorologist?
    - Playwright and Digital Marketing Copywriter?
    - Choreographer and Museum visitor experience designer?
- Bring In Around Beyond into your Career discussions to enable learners to explore their response to different Career choices.

Messages for learners

Careers choices can be very closely connected to my academic subjects, or quite distant

Careers choices that are close to my academic subjects will probably draw on a lot of Knowledge, whereas those which are less closely connected will offer me the chance to learn new things

Careers choices that are further away from my academic subjects will draw more on the Attributes and transferable Skills that I develop through studying those subjects than they will on any Knowledge

I will always be making decisions about my Career next steps in the same way: how closely do I want to build on and carry forward my Knowledge or do I want my Attributes, Skills, Experience, and enthusiasm for learning to help me move in a new direction?

Employability is not only something to do with work: it is the way to describe how everything I learn and develop – my Knowledge, Attributes, Skills, and Experience – through my education and beyond helps me gain and contribute value.

Notes

1 I want to acknowledge the brilliant work by Sue Moseley, Morag Walling, and Tisha Pryor, all Careers Consultants at King's College London, who between them originally piloted and developed this approach with students in the School of Bioscience Education to help them identify Careers choices related to their degree. I have adapted it here for a pre-18 audience and incorporated the Employability concepts outlined earlier in this chapter.
2 I have not included Teacher or Researcher in any of these categories, but they would of course be natural and valid choices for each of In, Around, and Beyond.

Part **4**

Overcoming the Challenges

So, let us revisit the Challenges I outlined in the opening sections.

Challenge 1: The Hourglass Phenomenon

This is addressed by talking about the relationship between academic study and Careers choices, by focusing on the different ways in which Employability assets are deployed.

- Knowledge, Attributes, Skills and Experience, Learning, and In Around Beyond give ways to understand the Employability value of qualifications and use them to explore future choices
- Explore Encounter Embark supports self-aware Careers decision-making.

Challenge 2: Qualifications as Knowledge Assets

This is addressed by exploring the other elements of qualifications that are developed through academic study, and understanding the difference between Knowledge and Learning.

- Learning, Attributes, Skills, and Experience provide a way to understand the Employability value of qualifications beyond Knowledge alone
- That feeds into Explore Encounter Embark and In Around Beyond for envisaging Careers journeys.

Challenge 3: Paralysis

This is addressed by understanding that each qualification offers multiple outcomes, but that is managed by exploring the connections between qualifications that are based on Attributes, Skills, and future Careers choices.

- Explore Encounter Embark offers learners a way to establish how the process fits with their Careers journey stage
- In Around Beyond shows the relationship between the Employability value of the qualifications on offer and future choices
- Possibilities are managed by connecting self-awareness of Attributes and Skills with self-awareness of the Careers journey stage, to narrow options as well as opening them up in a controlled way.

Challenge 4: Narrowing definitions of success

Diversifying definitions of success for learners is achieved through better understanding of the relationship between the subjects they study and the options opened up by the innate Attributes and Skills in those subjects.

- In Around Beyond enables learners to be aware of and control the relationships between subjects they choose, rather than having connections and choices forced upon them
- In conjunction with well-triaged information and experiences through Explore Encounter Embark, learners can take ownership of how they make decisions.

Challenge 5: The Neuroscience of the adolescent brain

We can't fix this, and nor should we!

Watching learners become who they are going to be, with all the opportunities, curiosity, mistakes, and uncertainties that are part of that, is one of the privileges of being an educator. But we can do so much more to support and enable how adolescent learners navigate their way through some of the decisions that feel risky to them, but need not be. And we can do this by using a few tools and processes to help you get far more benefit from what you all as incredibly hard-working Careers Leaders, Careers professionals, and teachers are already doing. This is not difficult or complicated thinking. Some good navigation gives learners the platform to create a clear Careers journey, and that is easily supported by strong self-awareness of how their education enables and lays the foundation for their transition into work through Knowledge, Attributes, Skills, and Experience. That gives learners the foundation to build the right future for them.

Part 5

Transitions

After all the opportunities you put in place to reflect and learn and try, there still comes a point when your learners move on to what is next. As with **Challenge 5**, I am not going to reinvent the wheel of neuroscientific research into the passage to adulthood, and I highly recommend Sarah-Jayne Blakemore's books on this topic. Instead in this section, I gather together some ideas to share with your learners to enable them to make successful transitions into whatever comes next for them. They draw on the same Attributes and transferable Skills that students develop during their curriculum learning, which I discussed in the Skills section of this book. And they are shaped around what students, recent graduates, and new employees tell me they wish they had known, before they made their transitions.

Before I started work, I wish I'd known ...

'... that senior managers are, more often than not, happy to talk to me!'

Learners are sometimes surprised to find that the structures of work are more like those of school and college than they expect. Emphasis is sometimes placed on how different work and education are, but that is not always true. In terms of structure, work often resembles pre-18 learning quite closely because of the relatively high levels of structure and supervision that scaffold the early working experiences. Learners often imagine that work will require long periods of working independently of supervision and possibly alone, and certainly new employees will be given space, time, and opportunity to develop their Skills and abilities and explore and acquire new Knowledge under their own control.

It is impossible and inappropriate to generalise, of course, because learners entering apprenticeship schemes will find a significant amount of structure imposed on the experience due to the criteria around progress and assessment, while others entering the workplace without a programme of development will find that routines and tasks are what provide the structure. But giving learners the opportunity to reflect in advance on what structure means to them, whether they like and welcome it, or feel challenged or restricted by it, will help them recognise it in work and decide how they are going to manage and respond well to it.

Structure also takes on different forms. It can shape the way in which a day is organised, in terms of different periods of activity. Learners entering construction trades may be surprised by the number of short breaks that can punctuate the day, but the work is physically arduous, and the coordination with deliveries and other trades, or the timings around concrete drying or glues setting, will affect how work ebbs and flows.

Structure can also shape the way in which the work is done, reflecting the need or ability to complete tasks in a linear or simultaneous fashion. A plumber, for example, will work progressively through a task until it is completed, while a legal executive may work on several tasks simultaneously because the timescale of completion is much longer. So, enabling learners to recognise the role of time and timescales in the structures of work, and sometimes to relate that to the familiar role of time and timescales in the structures of their education, can be a key step in preparing for transition to work.

Structure can shape the personal accountabilities of the new employee to managers and teams. Many organisations use meetings to share and discuss work, across different teams and one-to-one relationships. To a new employee, this might seem like a lot of unnecessary chat (and sometimes it is!) but it is also how projects are discussed, improved, and progressed. It also helps learners to understand that, unlike education, many roles and sectors create products and services that cannot be made by individuals in isolation. The transferable Skill of teamwork is a bit of a cliché when it comes to talking about work, but it is fundamental to many roles and sectors, from laboratory research where findings are analysed and evaluated, to marketing where creative approaches are brainstormed, to product design where ideas are tested and refined.

Structure also reflects organisational and external hierarchies and accountabilities. Whether the organisation is large or small, and both in apprenticeships and work that does not have programmes of development, everyone is accountable to someone. In a small business or self-employed apprenticeship context, the 'boss' is also possibly the person that the new employee is learning from and alongside. That accountability can feel far more direct than joining a huge global professional services firm as a trainee accountant, where the senior Partners in the business are dozens of layers above in the organisation. But in almost every context, there is client accountability too. Pretty much all work is for someone. Often new employees will meet the client directly: this is the case in small business and self-employed trades. But global professional services firms also work 'for someone' and a new employee might find their first meetings with clients to be overwhelming and almost alien. Everyone else in the room looks like they know why they are there, and the meeting seems to follow some mysterious plan that everyone else seems to understand. Getting to grips with this is simply about coming to terms with the structures, which, in the end, are often not that unlike those of classes in education:

- Why are we here? (What did we learn last time?)
- Where are we up to in this project? (Today's class will be about …)
- What are the problems we want to solve today, that we need to talk about together? (This is the new content, and what you are going to learn to do with it)
- What steps are we going to take now to progress this? (Practice, reflection, understanding, progress).

We call them meetings, but they are all about establishing, creating, and charting progress.

So, we can support learners to prepare to experience new structures effectively in work by helping them recognise the role played by the Attributes and Skills they have already developed in education. These might include:

Attributes

- curiosity
- seeing the bigger picture
- respecting others
- being appropriately assertive.

Skills

- Research – get to know their organisation and workplaces
- Observation – recognise the underlying structure in a situation, understand interrelationships in teams and activities
- Analysis – identify problems and opportunities, make connections, challenge assumptions.

'... that the opportunities that matter are not just in the short term but also the mid term'

This brings us to how the new employee identifies their own progress in work. Programmes of workplace development, such as apprenticeships, should make it very clear to the new employee what the goals are, what the markers on the journey look like, and how progress is being evaluated. In that respect, an apprenticeship can resemble pre-18 education quite closely, although the timescales are often much shorter for stages of progress. A well-structured programme should give the new employee or apprentice a really strong sense of their progress through the programme, but also frequent opportunities to recognise and reflect positively on what new Knowledge and Skills they are developing. They may be directly assessed on this in order to demonstrate that, but when you are discussing apprenticeships with learners, it is also useful to emphasise that moving into work involves taking more responsibility for their own progress, not just learning to do new things well, but also being able to recognise their own competence and confidence. That becomes really important to minimise the potential for things going wrong and new employees struggling; unlike pre-18 education, where there is usually someone actively looking out for strugglers and stragglers, that may not be the case in a work environment, particularly if there is minimal one-to-one supervision.

It may also be more difficult for recent employees or apprentices to admit they are finding new things hard, particularly when the pace of learning and change seems higher. Workplaces do not stream or group new employees together by ability or aptitude in the way that can occur in some aspects of pre-18 education: if a learner has got a place on a scheme, it is assumed that they have the potential to learn and the ability to keep up. That is why self-awareness becomes so important so quickly in the workplace. Managers, supervisors, and apprenticeship programme leaders will expect and rely on learners to be able to identify for themselves where they are doing well and where they are finding progress more challenging, and while a learner in college might have been able to avoid thinking about it in the expectation that a conscientious teacher will spot it and respond, that is far less likely to happen in the workplace. That can be very paralysing for new employees, and it is one of the reasons that learners often choose higher education instead of work, believing that it will be easier to make that transition to taking responsibility in work for themselves and their progress when they are older. Unfortunately, self-awareness – like personal fitness – needs conscious work and attention all the time so, as we will find out in the chapter about higher education, the responsibility for assessing their own progress does fall to the new employee, sooner or later.

I would encourage you to help learners recognise that taking responsibility for their progress is not something to be afraid of or reluctant about. In other contexts – mastering sports Skills or a musical instrument, creative activities, making money in an enterprise project or side gig – they quickly recognise and own their successes and aspire to more. That does also happen in learning, of course, in terms of progress in understanding something difficult. So, it can help to anchor learners' understanding of self-awareness and progress in the familiar first, before they leave school or college, and help them recognise what success feels like to them, as well as what it looks like in abstract.

Recognising one's own progress is something we all have to do, throughout our working lives, and people have different interests in progress. If work is a matter of subsistence and not reward, then progress is sometimes less important to an individual than for those who find it stimulating and a key part of their identity and definitions of success. Progress in the former context is often less about learning to do more complex tasks or take on more responsibility, and more about managing the unexpected without stress or difficulty or playing a part in maintaining a contented and effective workplace community. Progress comes to mean very different things to different people, but helping learners recognise that it is a way in which work is calibrated, particularly for new employees (how quickly have you picked this up?, can you be deployed into other tasks?, can you be relied on to take the initiative?, etc.), is helpful for making a good transition into work.

For learners who see entering work at 16 or 18 as an opportunity to get ahead, helping them learn how to set goals both within a programme and independently is important. In a digital culture which feels very immediate and short-termist, and which is strongly shaped by apparently successful and relatively young people close to learners' ages, learners often end up setting very unrealistic goals for what success will look like and the timescales for it. They may also struggle to reconcile the imposed structures and progressions of a scheme with their own imaginative ambitions, ideas, and activities, so giving learners a space to discuss those tensions openly is valuable. For example, the learner who has designed an app and is making a bit of money from it, but is also doing an apprenticeship in software development, may feel that they know already more from their own experiences than they are learning on the programme. This quickly leads to frustration, so helping learners recognise in advance how the bigger picture is made up of these two paths as complementary, and not in conflict, will help them identify where gain through the programme is an advantage and easier than trying to achieve the same outcome independently. This is also a way to introduce learners to the idea of compromise and offsetting: when does a gain in one area mean a compromise in another? And when can seeing the bigger picture help me come to terms with individual frustrations? Again, this all contributes to a sense of progress.

So, we can support learners to prepare to evaluate their progress effectively in work by helping them recognise the role played by the Attributes and Skills they have already developed in education. These might include:

Attributes

- autonomy
- self-management
- shaping their own growth
- taking the initiative
- patience.

Skills

- Analysis – apply analysis of others' work to develop my own work, interpret observations, interpret results, draw comparisons, understand the nature of change and of causation
- Observation – identify patterns in outputs or processes and recognise relationships within those patterns, make and record observations, gather evidence
- Communication – summarise information concisely, question effectively, summarise others' views, receive feedback constructively.

'... that being proactive pays off'

Which leads to a discussion about responsibility. There are life factors that surface quickly for some when they enter work, such as moving away from home, leaving care, or having to contribute financially to the family. Hopefully, your school or college is helping learners with these topics in PSHE classes or something similar, and there are good resources online to help learners come to terms with what life Skills they will need to develop.

In this context though, I am considering responsibility as a counter to accountability: accountability for the work is to others, responsibility for the work is to oneself. I will explore workplace behaviours and professionalism as a type of responsibility in a later section, but here I want to reflect on the responsibility of the individual to themselves to commit to work as a next Career step, and also to recognise when things are not what they want or what they should be.

No one wants someone else to be unhappy in work. We have all worked with colleagues who felt they were in the wrong job, or were deeply unhappy despite being successful. As peers we feel a responsibility to others to enable them to resolve their problems and find success that is more meaningful to them. But as the neuroscience in **Challenge 5** indicates, younger employees generally lack the experiential learning and reference points to draw on to know whether something is hard but worth sticking at despite frustration, or is genuinely making them miserable and is a poor choice.

Again, the value of self-awareness is central here, and it is where good reflective habits really help learners when they are transitioning into work. We can forearm learners with questions that they reflect on before they leave education, that they can keep coming back to in work:

- What is my definition of success – on a daily basis, but also a week-by-week or month-by-month basis?
- What is my goal here, notwithstanding possible challenges of this job?
- Why did I think this was a good choice for me originally?
  - Has that reasoning changed – do I now know something about this choice that I didn't know before?
  - Or has something in me changed – do I now know something about myself that I didn't know before?

I cannot reiterate strongly enough the importance of learners knowing that there is no such thing as a bad decision. There are decisions we wish in hindsight we had not made, because work was challenging or the learning was not what we wanted, or we discovered we were not suited to something, or because the journey is now going to be a bit more meandering or take longer, or because we were miserable. But we learn so much that is valuable about ourselves and what is important from all of those experiences, even if we wish that we had not gained that learning negatively. Furthermore, our ability to cope with the challenges and difficulties that arise in every job is strengthened enormously by previous challenges and difficulties. If you have always made a perfect decision and been successful without difficulties, you will have very little experience to draw on when problems become larger and more complex to resolve. This can be the challenge that learners who have been channelled into a particular decision can find later on: without other reference points to draw on, they struggle when they meet the unexpected. And in this unpredictable, fluid, and challenging pandemic-shaped world, we need to encourage learners to recognise how all learning helps them become more resilient and able to make better decisions.

So, the learner who becomes a new employee or apprentice has so much responsibility to themselves, not least because if they have not taken that seriously, they will find it more difficult to meet their accountabilities to others, and to help their supervisors and managers recognise when they are struggling or not enjoying the work.

On the positive side, it is equally important that learners recognise when they are enjoying what they are doing, how they develop new definitions of success in different contexts, how to recognise small achievements as building blocks in a bigger picture of progress. And how all these things add up to the self-awareness of a decision having been well made with a positive outcome. Learners whose experiences and definitions of success have been framed by tests, exams, and qualifications often lack alternative ways to frame good outcomes in a work context. In many schemes there will be exams and qualifications, but they are not present day by day, and, once qualified, progress in a Career path and the responsibility to oneself for success can seem suddenly very ambiguous. This is one of the key transitions, in my opinion, from jumping through process and procedural hoops to choosing and shaping one's own hoops. The conversations you have with your learners will help establish good habits of decision-making and self-awareness that matter and sustain us throughout life, wherever it takes us.

So, we can support learners to prepare to take responsibility for themselves effectively in work by helping them recognise the role played by the Attributes and Skills they have already developed in education. These might include:

Attributes

- adaptability
- emotional intelligence
- self-awareness
- awareness of my strengths and development areas
- enthusiasm.

Skills

- Creativity – select ideas for exploration, design a range of approaches to achieve specific objectives
- Observation – identify opportunities in different contexts, make and record observations
- Analysis – interpret observations, evaluate risks, refine ideas, think critically, weigh available options, make decisions.

'... that building strong relationships with my manager gives me the honest, constructive feedback that helps build my Career'

This leads to how we can enable learners to recognise the support mechanisms that will be present in and around the workplace. Formal structures both in organisational hierarchy and programme design will offer certain types of support mechanisms and processes, such as supervisors and managers in the workplace and educators and professionals in the training provider. In some respects these will resemble the support structures of education, but in other respects they will not. Again, it is impossible to generalise, but something learners may recognise is that reflective opportunities may be less structured and that they may need to take more responsibility for bringing their own questions and concerns to those in support roles around them. In a very small organisation or self-employment apprenticeship such as in the construction trade, the apprentice might generally work with the same person all the time, so they may feel there is not really anyone else to talk to about how they are getting on, or when they are finding things difficult. Encourage learners to find out from their training provider at the start of the scheme how to raise questions and any concerns, and what expectations they can have of support from those they will be working with. It is always better to be prepared than have to work that out in a crisis.

There is also likely to be a difference in what kind of support is available. Unlike education where there is an approach to pastoral care that infuses schools and colleges, the workplace will not offer that in the same structured way. I am sure many of us have been contacted by recent leavers who are finding things more challenging than they expected, and feel they do not have anyone else to turn to for reflecting and figuring out what to do. If you do not already have one, you may want to set up a recent alumni group, particularly for those entering work, so they have peers to draw on – and if you want to be involved, you can work with them as a group: more on that in the next section. Some training providers may offer a Careers professional as part of the learning community: we all recognise that our interactions with learners are often about far more than just future working lives, and the personal experiences of the individual are rightly a part of those journeys and discussions. But it might also be helpful to give learners access to information about how to access mental health support, other support services, as well as trade unions and professional bodies before they leave your school or college, so they recognise that there is a larger ecosystem of support which they are going to enter as adults.

Regrettably, some apprentices and new employees will only seek help and support when they are at crisis point, such as failing an assessment or being given a warning about inadequate performance or accountabilities that have not been met. For the new employee, these moments can be shattering and deeply disheartening. They might not be unexpected but the realisation can be disruptive that they cannot ignore their instincts or external warning signs. These situations can also feel like dead ends in terms of Career journeys, and can damage decision-making confidence. They are not, however, generally irretrievable, and you can enable learners to prepare well to enter work both by familiarising themselves with where the structural pressure points might be (particularly in organised schemes) but also to recognise where the behavioural pressure points might be (more on that below). Whatever the role, sector, or level of responsibility, proactivity is generally a key mindset in ensuring everything goes smoothly.

So, we can support learners to prepare to identify and take advantage of the support around them in work by helping them recognise the role played by the Attributes and Skills they have already developed in education. These might include:

Attributes

- aware of my community
- responsible for my own actions
- emotional intelligence
- self-reflective
- being aware of the bigger picture.

Skills

- Organisation and planning
- Analysis – identify risks, understand the nature of consequence, identify, break down and solve problems
- Communication – express own views, listen effectively, question effectively, build relationships.

'... that work is a human environment, so I should take care in how I interact with others'

In work, peers are as much a part of the support network as they are in education, and peer networks also expand as existing networks remain in some form while new networks evolve. In work, relationship networks will be distributed across a wider range of ages and profiles, and new employees and apprentices will find themselves in mixed groups working on a project, or meeting clients from very different backgrounds and perspectives. This is another key area of transition, as young people understand more about the complexities of society and figure out what their contribution is going to be. Again, your school or college is likely to be considering these issues in civic and social education classes, but work can often feel like a more pressurised environment in which to have to make judgements about situations and understand social and professional cues from others.

Peers of a similar age or situation can therefore offer a valuable network for figuring out some of this 'extra-curricular' learning about workplace dynamics and personal relationships and partnerships. But these networks are also for giving as well as receiving, in the sense that sharing self-reflection and perspectives not only helps the individual but others too. Larger organisations may have active learning sets or cohorts of entrants who meet regularly for discussion, but that is not on offer in small businesses or with self-employed professionals. New employees will often turn to the social media and online space for help and perspective, so, as above, you may want to set up a recent alumni group online, particularly for those entering work, so they have peers to draw on. If you have capacity or want to be involved, you can work with them as a group by structuring discussion boards with key questions, or organising thirty-minute online catch-ups in lunchbreak or after work time for alumni to get together and catch up. It is tempting to make these feel formal and educational, but for many new employees it will be an opportunity to let off steam with each other about work and process new experiences. You can maintain a listening role that creates a safe space and offers perspective when needed. But you can also ask older alumni to host groups and forums like this; the wisdom of someone who has already been down the same road has significant value.

It is tempting and perhaps inevitable that new employees and apprentices will compare themselves to their peers when they get together, or perhaps exaggerate one way or the other. So, try to reinforce the focus on individuals having their own definitions of success, and being honest about their experiences. There is no weakness in reflecting honestly, and that self-awareness is necessary in the workplace. Comparison of an experience can quickly turn into comparisons of happiness or quantifiable successes, when a more productive focus can be self-awareness and recognition of change and growth. After an education where they have all had broadly similar experiences, new employees can be a bit overwhelmed or disorientated by the diversity of experiences they have in their peer group. Notwithstanding a failure by an employer to deliver appropriately to an employee, there is no right or wrong here but peers sometimes need some support to recognise that. Likewise, peers can sometimes hear transformative messages of encouragement, persistence, or empowerment from each other that they cannot hear from us or other more experienced figures.

So we can support learners to prepare to identify and take advantage of their peer communities by helping them recognise the role played by the Attributes and Skills they have already developed in education. These might include:

Attributes

- respect others
- act to benefit others
- be empathetic
- be truthful
- be open-minded.

Skills

- Communication – express ideas with nuance, express own views, listen effectively, question effectively, make accurate references, build rapport, give constructive feedback.

'... to prepare for structured conversations with my manager so I don't waste their time ... and always double-check my work!'

Which brings us to workplace professionalism and appropriate behaviours. No employer is going to expect the finished article to turn up on the first day of work, in terms of professionalism and workplace awareness. But they will expect a new employee to understand why professionalism is important, and they will expect to see some sensitivity to change and appropriateness.

Professionalism means something very different on a construction site, in a hospital, a retail setting, or a bank in terms of the observances of the processes and procedures of that workplace. There will also be huge latitude in how much control or rigidity there is in those processes. But professionalism also means some commonly understood behaviours like punctuality, respect, awareness of accountabilities and responsibilities, and context-appropriate communication which transcend roles and sectors. Some of these overlap with life Skills while others seem more unfamiliar, and for learners who choose work at 16 or 18 because they perceive it as a striking alternative to education, it can be disappointing or unsettling to see some shared priorities and perceived regulation of behaviour.

In a workplace setting, however, professionalism is more about common good and consequences, and this can be a good way to introduce learners to that transition before it happens. For example, turning up late to a school lesson does not significantly impact or hold up other learners, while turning up late to a client meeting or a healthcare patient interaction can have serious consequences such as loss of business or loss of opportunity for the patient for treatment. Others are impacted by that choice and behaviour. And this may be the first time that new employees encounter those sorts of accountabilities.

Many organisations or professions have codes of conduct and professional competences that incorporate basic operational behaviours, commercial context expectations, and other competences, so new employees and apprentices may find themselves formally introduced to those early on. Likewise, some workplaces require certain procedures and processes to be followed for health and safety reasons, which also embeds an understanding. But the key narrative for learners to understand is that professionalism is not just about 'my behaviours' but also about the impact of my behaviours on others. In the transition to the working world, understanding that you are now one of many in a complex ecosystem of moving parts, whether a self-employed carpenter's apprentice or an ambulance practitioner or a legal apprentice in a nationwide firm, is one of the most important new perspectives to recognise and act on.

So, we can support learners to develop by helping them recognise the role played by the Attributes and Skills they have already developed in education. These might include:

Attributes

- diligence
- self-discipline
- respect for others
- appreciate consequences of my actions
- integrity.

Skills

- Creativity – create new approaches to improving performance, make appropriate use of relevant conventions
- Analysis – understand the impact of context, identify and describe how impact, attitudes, and values are created and conveyed, identify subtle differences with wider impacts, understand the nature of causation and of consequence, follow instructions, weigh options, evaluate risks
- Communication – receive feedback constructively, listen effectively, use appropriate language, understand how audience influences interpretation.

A note on digital Skills and the workplace

I want to conclude this section about the transition to work by noting the role of digital Skills. There have been plenty of media stories since the start of the pandemic about the digital Skills gap, and the transformation in the use of digital platforms in study and work has significantly accelerated the need for the development of these Skills in learners. Digital education research and scholarship have already identified that younger people's interactions with digital technologies are 'restructuring and extending young people's mental faculties and ability to learn'.[1] What that means for learners' future engagement with work – and indeed how they may go on to shape work for other generations already in the workplace – will be fascinating. However, in the meantime there are some assumptions which I think learners are often not aware of, and which are worth exploring here as part of considering transition.

It's a small world

Many learners are better connected than ever due to the migration of learning online, but you will also be all too aware of the impacts of digital poverty, which, after all, is an extension of actual poverty. Employers and universities are aware of this too, and there is increased focus on what needs to be done to support apprentices and students to get access to what they need in order to continue with their professional and academic development. There is continued challenging of the assumption that every learner is online, and a recognition that having a smart phone to access the world wide web is not a platform for an effective learning experience in work or study. The solutions are still some way off, but it is a topic of active consideration.

That said, it is helpful for learners to recognise that digital and online learning is likely to become a significant and permanent part of how work and education take place, in absolute and blended forms. The pandemic has accelerated aspects of the Fourth Industrial Revolution in terms of communications platforms, workplace connectivity, and task operation. Many organisations that previously were separated by geography are now more closely connected, and learners joining the workplace in a number of sectors may find in the future that they are working with other apprentices around the country through online delivery by training providers. The traditional models of learning will change and learners will find themselves perhaps on the cutting edge of new approaches. This can seem off-putting – who wants to be a guinea pig? But in an employment landscape where tolerance for uncertainty and a flexible mindset are going to be key, being part of a wave of innovation, and taking the opportunity to shape that through interaction and feedback, is one of the best places to be.

Everyone enters work with the same level of digital capability

That is not true for digital or any other Skills or Knowledge, particularly at the ages of 16 or 18, or even later. While employers looking for experienced staff might reasonably expect applicants to have core levels of capability, that is not true for those starting work for the first time. What employers do look for is the potential to learn new ways of working, and they provide lots of training to develop that potential. It is not unreasonable to expect learners to have some awareness of different platforms or digital tools in word-processing, presentation, or web software, but if they specifically want that Knowledge or Skillset, they will ask for it. But it is important for learners to understand the constant presence of digital platforms in work and to recognise that almost all roles will develop some sort of digital competences.

All jobs require specialist digital Skillsets

That is also not true, but there are packages that are common to many types of roles. It can help to differentiate between basic functionality packages like MS Office and specialist tools like computer aided design, statistical analysis, or customer relationship management platforms.

As the number of learners with the ability to code increases, it is likely that a distinction will develop around those who can code and those who cannot that may extend beyond the IT sector. One of the features of the pandemic is the explosion in digital platforms across all areas of life (work, retail, entertainment) and if the innovations following the 2008 recession are an indicator, there will be a further wave of creative innovation in IT beyond the IT sector. It seems likely that in the future, employers will seek new employees who can code, to help them shape the business and respond creatively to challenges from within the organisation rather than relying on the IT sector to do that for them. That is not to say that all learners should have coding Skills – though that seems likely to happen anyway – but more to recognise that our understanding of core literacies in the workplace is likely to expand.

Everyone has the same level of digital capability in work

Again, they do not. As with all sorts of other Skills and academic disciplines, everyone is good at different things. New employees and apprentices will find that other people's Skills sit across a range of different types. That means finding their own niche is helpful to recognising how to build confidence and which tasks they might be able to complete quickly. All-round digital competence will grow and develop, and if new employees or apprentices feel they are lacking in a key area like spreadsheet Skills, most training providers and employers will be able to access online courses for them.

Being online is all the same, isn't it?

Learners can find it difficult to recognise that the way they operate in the digital world is very different to the way that work is done in the digital world. Young people are likely to communicate socially in images, shorthand, and instant messaging. It is visual, quick, and temporary. But the workplace tends to be a world of process, record, documentation, depth, words and data. In some ways, it could not be more opposite. The world of work will evolve and adapt, and it seems likely that the dominance of video conferencing has repositioned the visual and concise instant messaging in relation to email. Video and audio are increasingly present in how we pick up new information, so the diversification of communication styles is inevitable too. Learners are likely to shape this new digital language as well as being shaped by the way it used to be, so it will help to recognise the difference.

Digital Skills are more important than transferable Skills

If we consider the ability to use technology as a specialist Skillset, and include use of different software and coding as part of that Skillset, then there is no doubting that whether we are exiting a pandemic characterised by the shift to online learning and engagement or entering the Fourth Industrial Revolution, digital Skills are part of our infrastructure of study and work. But it is also really important to recognise that the acquisition, development, and deployment of digital Skills are strongly underpinned by Attributes and transferable Skills, for example, curiosity, creativity, approaching a process systematically, and solving problems. So, there is significant value in working with learners to help them understand how to use their Attributes and transferable Skills to ensure they develop and use their digital Skills effectively. Here are two examples and some associated questions that you can discuss with learners:

- Communication
  - Why does it matter more than ever to present well and interact effectively in the digital space?
  - What does teamwork mean in a digital workplace?
  - How do we build relationships when all our meetings are online and we don't connect informally in the same way?
- Organisation and Self-Management
  - How do I manage my time when digital tools schedule everything?
  - How do I manage intensity from staring at a screen all day?

- How do I manage my work independently when my manager is not nearby?
- How do I manage working alone when I'm not in the workplace with others?

Note

1 See Neil Selwyn's reference to the work of Greenfield and of Prensky in Selwyn, N. (2017) *Education and Technology: Key issues and debates*, 2nd edition. London: Bloomsbury, p. 72.

Before I started university, I wish I'd known ...

'... that structure and routine come with practice. Going to university is about adjusting to a new way of doing things and finding your own rhythm'

You will know from your own experience of university that different degree courses offer vastly different learning structures, in terms of contact time with academics and peers, independent study, group work, practical work, and assessment styles. These also differ by institution type, with some universities offering compulsory whole-of-first-year courses and others offering embedded work-based learning. Some courses take a very interdisciplinary approach with modular structures enabling considerable curriculum flexibility, while others are rigidly structured according to the requirements of Professional Standards and Regulatory Bodies (e.g. nursing, medicine, dentistry).

All these factors will offer both contrast and similarity to further education, and students can find it helpful to consider structure when they are making choices about what to study. Many humanities students are shocked by an apparent imbalance between academic contact time and independent study, because they have not considered one of the key shifts in learning relates to them developing their own critical perspectives and voices. Pre-18 teaching and learning styles rarely offer the capacity for learners to try this out, through no fault of teachers, so helping learners really understand what such a difference means in practice can be difficult.

So, as a Careers Leader, Careers professional, or a teacher you will be working with learners who may have to create 80 per cent of their own structure, alongside those whose schedules will be so tightly constructed around lectures, seminars, and laboratory work that they barely have time to get to the library. How can we best prepare all these learners for what is coming?

One key message is to help all learners recognise that independent learning is a fundamental feature of university, whatever course they are on. Even after a heavily scheduled day, a student will still have to decide how to prioritise research, assignments, practice, review, groupwork preparation, tidying or organising notes, and so on. They may have less time for that than a Philosophy or English Literature student, but the tasks remain the same. The same Skills of good study apply, and every university will offer courses or advice on Study

Skills and Research Skills to help learners understand what is expected. However, these expectations are not explicitly measured or assessed. A lecturer or tutor may ask a first-year student about their study habits, but they may not.

So, there is no accountability as such; the only evidence comes when the student submits an assignment or sits an examination, and the infrastructure that supports them to reach that goal successfully is put under pressure. Inaccurate note-taking, poor time management, disorganisation, and an incomplete picture of what has been studied will all add vulnerabilities to the student's ability to demonstrate what they have learned. Thus, while it may seem tiresome to repeat school behaviours in higher education, they are there for good reason and this time no teacher will be peering over their shoulder, frowning at the graffiti on a notebook.

We could also argue that those accountabilities do surface later on when the graduate enters work. Most employers will assume that a student who has successfully graduated did so on the basis of sound self-organisation and self-management, and that they are capable of working independently without supervision. It seems paradoxical, but sometimes recognising the absence of structure in higher education, and formulating a practical response to that, orm one of the key benefits to a student in the longer term.

Recognising this contrast in structures can also be helpful in enabling new students to respond to and reshape their own personal behaviours. For example, when you just have one final deadline for an essay, how do you balance leaving enough time to have read everything that might be useful with allowing enough time to draft and re-draft a good essay? In abstract, this is a challenge for both the well-prepared and the procrastinator! Likewise, for a student who feels excited but also overwhelmed by entering a huge new social community and immediately has to join students from lots of different programmes on a multidisciplinary course, the imposition of expected structures of interaction and delivery can feel terrifying to begin with.

It is important to acknowledge how incredibly overwhelming the start of a new degree course can be. There is a huge volume of information and experience being funnelled towards new students in the first three or four weeks, and particularly in a fully or partially online learning context it can be very difficult for new students to get their bearings on how their experience should be structured and how they should structure it. That is why it can really help learners planning to go to university to focus on all the other non-social aspects, and to talk to alumni who have studied their chosen subjects about how to create a good foundation.

So, we can support learners to prepare for presence and absence of structure in higher education by helping them recognise the role played by the Attributes and Skills they have already developed. These might include:

Attributes

- growth mindset
- learn independently

- self-direct
- intellectually curious.

Skills

- Create – design a range of approaches to achieve specific objectives
- Observation – recognise the underlying structure in a situation, record experiences and observations in a variety of ways
- Research – structure research processes
- Analysis – identify problems and opportunities, challenge assumptions, evaluate risks, explore connections within and across subject areas.

'... that I should check my own sense of progress against that of other students, and get the perspective of the academics and tutors'

In the context of a range of different structures, students will be given very different frames of reference to evaluate their progress in understanding. The topics of the course may be very clearly spelled out in the course virtual learning environment, and the pile of notes may grow ever larger, but in subjects where learners need to bring more structure of their own to their learning experience, it can seem really difficult to figure out how well they are doing.

Students may not recognise lectures and seminars as opportunities to check up on their own progress. Lectures tend to be about the introduction of new content and ideas, while seminars are for reflection, but when students are focused on the immediate task at hand ('Have I read the right articles for this week?'), they can often and easily lose track of the bigger picture of how the readings fit together or why the course has been structured in the way it has. Lectures can, however, be seen as beacons or way markers on the course journey, and students who are developing their independent learning and thinking Skills should consider why particular topics have been chosen for a lecture sequence. Seminars or any group discussion, whether with peers or with academics or research students, provide not only an opportunity to check that this week's reading has been understood but also to explore connections between this and other content. Students may not realise this until some way into their first term, by which time it is too late to benefit from the early opportunities to get their bearings. That is particularly true in humanities disciplines, while in subjects where Knowledge is interdependent, particularly sciences or disciplines where specialist Skills are progressively developed and applied (e.g. creativity and design), it can be easier to track the cause and effect ('I needed to know that before I learned to do this').

Students can also create their own sense of progress by adopting a proactive perspective on their syllabus, particularly now most universities are using some sort of virtual learning environment to store and present course information. Why has the course been structured in this way? What can be deduced about why the key topics have been presented in this order? What do the assessments suggest about what I am expected to understand at each assessment point? Courses with formative assessment are particularly useful for that reflection, and those which have a lot of formative assessment in them, such as weekly multiple choice tests, blogs, or practice questions, are built for continuous reflection on progress. As with the seminars, it is helpful for new students to recognise that these are not just opportunities to pass or fail, but also to build confidence that they can see how all that they are studying fits together.

All courses will include elements of feedback, whether from formative assessments, seminar interactions, or meetings with academic or pastoral tutors. It is very much in universities' interests to ensure that their learners do well in the course and progress from year to year, so they all take proactive measures to identify students who are struggling. That said, students do need to define their own early-warning signs that help them recognise for themselves if they are having difficulty keeping up or feel they have misunderstood key concepts. As with the variability of structure, variability of contact and assessment points can make students feel that they do not know how they are doing, and if they rely too much on assessment points, it may be too late to get the help they need to get back on track.

Early-warning signs might include having trouble focusing on study, having difficulty finding the right books or sources for clarifying information, avoiding certain classes, not being clear about what is expected in a piece of work, feeling confused in a discussion. All of these are also completely normal responses when a topic is new, on top of being in a new environment and making new friends. So, key is recognising that the situation is not improving, and that one or more of these issues keeps happening. Students should reach out to their named personal tutor, to their seminar tutor, or even to the administrator for their course or department, who will help them find the right person to speak to. There is no shame in taking time to get to grips with what is new, and it will help a lot if the student can show that they have tried to put good approaches to study and learning in place.

Students will also derive an element of feedback from seminars or groupwork. For some students it can be difficult to avoid a sense of competition in these settings, and there will always be confident students who enjoy the opportunity to explore publicly what they know and test ideas that they have discovered. Others may find this form of public discussion very challenging and it can be easy to feel at a disadvantage. A good seminar will enable everyone to contribute and feel respected on their learning journey, but it is sensible for students to find other ways to have those reflective conversations on the content. Finding other peers as study buddies, forming small study groups of their own, or taking advantage of peer mentoring schemes that many universities now offer for study will all help students hear a diverse range of points of view, and develop their own critical thinking and communication Skills. It can be difficult, sometimes, to remember that higher education is about the learning journey and not the destination. That makes it different to pre-18 education, and it is the development of those transferable Skills in that journey that employers are seeking.

The ultimate demonstration of progress is, inevitably, the mark at the end of a module, the end of the year, and the final degree classification. But as with any subject, degree programmes are made up of different types of disciplinary Knowledge and Skills. Not all students are equally good at all of them, and university is perhaps the first place where students will begin to see how much Knowledge and Skills are differentiated within a subject. They may have thought during GCSE Mathematics that they were better at geometry and vectors than algebra, and not realised that they enjoyed the spatial and visual aspects of maths more than the manipulative aspects. But at university that definition of disciplines into core and optional or elective areas of Knowledge surfaces some of those different aspects more obviously. So, it helps learners to understand that at university their grades will also reflect the mosaic of different types of learning and Knowledge and Skills in the discipline. And some will be up and others might be down. Finding your strength and growing it to develop it as your specialism is one of the rewards of higher education.

So, we can support learners to prepare to evaluate their progress effectively in work by helping them recognise the role played by the Attributes and Skills they have already developed in education. These might include:

Attributes

- autonomy
- self-management
- curiosity
- share learning endeavour
- persistence.

Skills

- Creativity – create new approaches to improving performance
- Analysis – apply analysis of others' work to develop my own work, interpret observations, interpret results, draw comparisons, understand the nature of change and of causation
- Observation – identify patterns in outputs or processes and recognise relationships within those patterns, make and record observations, gather evidence
- Communication – summarise information concisely, question effectively, summarise others' views, receive feedback constructively.

'... that I needed to learn to listen to that little voice inside me with honesty, but also with challenge'

Unlike choosing to go into the workplace, higher education is – to be very frank – often chosen by learners as a delaying tactic. As discussed in **Challenges 3** and **5**, the paralysing impact of a lack of reference points other than school or college education often reinforces the view learners have of themselves that they are not ready for work. Retreating into what they perceive as the familiar can be presented as a sensible positive choice, though in many respects it is simply delaying the inevitable choice about the workplace that will happen three, four, or five years later. That choice will only be easier if something has changed in how the student understands themselves and their options.

This is the obvious part of the book for me to sound the trumpet about university Careers Services, and of course they are there to address exactly this situation. They provide multiple ways for students to get the information they need, explore their options, reflect on their choices in safe and well-supported conversations, try out new experiences, and decide how they are going to present themselves to future employers once their choice is made. Many universities use a three- or four-stage Careers journey model, and some also align Careers and Employability activities to the year of study. There are work-based learning schemes, credit-bearing internships, input from employers and problem-based learning, workplace visits and employer Skills sessions, as well as events, panels, and practical projects. Alumni contribute too, so there is a huge range of perspectives and input to help students develop and take responsibility for their future Careers choices.

It is therefore no surprise that I strongly recommend that students get into the Careers Service as soon as they can after starting at university, find out what is on offer, and reflect on where they most need the help. If they self-identify as Explore, then Career planning workshops, one-to-one discussion, part-time work, alumni panels, and online reflective learning will help the student get to know what they are interested in, what typical destinations graduates go on to, and how to start recognising what Skills and Attributes they are developing through their course. Encounter students will look for opportunities to experience the workplace in different ways, perhaps as part of their course or through volunteering, and will start using what they learn from employer events and their research to narrow down their options. Embark students will be refining their CVs and applications, drawing on detailed conversations during employer fairs Skills sessions, and developing effective ways to talk about what they offer and what they have learned. Support for all these activities is available through the Careers Service, who increasingly in most universities are also partnering directly with academic departments.

But even with this infrastructure of support in place, students do need to take personal responsibility for their Careers exploration and decision-making. While working towards the degree result is naturally the priority, research and data show that students who graduate with a plan for their next Career step are more likely to get a good job after they leave university. There is also value to students in gaining other perspectives from outside study during study; the ability to take account of and incorporate diverse points of view is core to so many jobs and Careers, and this is a strong benefit of balancing study with work. I mentioned earlier that Experience of the workplace is fundamental to making decisions well, and employers increasingly expect that students will have some sort of workplace experience before applying for a scheme or role.

Using a Three Stage Careers Journey in your school or college therefore lays a foundation for the next cycle of this reflective journey when your learners get to university. And while over the course of their studies they may go round and round that cycle several times while they figure out what they want to do, they are already taking responsibility for making their own progress on that journey.

But we all – teachers, Careers professionals, students, academics, employers – want students to really enjoy their degree too. As I have said to academic colleagues many times, we do want the same thing: that students will love their degree and derive longer-term value from it in different ways. Even if a student does not make a choice about their next Career step before they graduate, they should leave being able to talk with passion and commitment about what they have studied, why they enjoyed it, and what the transferable and wider value of it is. That is essential for all students, particularly those who have chosen university to delay thinking about something else, and they should be encouraged from the outset to own their decision to study with that same passion and commitment.

So, we can support learners to prepare to take responsibility for themselves effectively while at university by helping them recognise the role played by the Attributes and Skills they have already developed – and will continue to develop – in education. These might include:

Attributes

- aspiring
- shape my own growth
- self-awareness
- awareness of my strengths and development areas
- enthusiasm.

Skills

- Creativity – select ideas for exploration, respond to own and other perspectives, design a strategy defining outcomes, approaches and decisions required
- Observation – record experiences and observations in a variety of ways, identify opportunities in different contexts

- Research – generate and explore lines of enquiry
- Analysis – evaluate different explanations, develop perspectives, evaluate risks, refine ideas, think critically, weigh available options, make decisions.

'... that universities are generally well set up to support me, but I should reach out for help *before* I start feeling overwhelmed to take good care of myself'

I mentioned in the section on progress the range of reference points that are available to students in the context of their academic study. Academic departments are focused on the academic well-being of students, and are acutely aware of the stresses students experience when they enter this new environment. Furthermore, all higher education professionals are deeply aware of the vulnerability of student mental health, and universities are taking an increasingly detailed and nuanced approach to identifying, preventing, and addressing mental health issues experienced by students.

All universities will have some sort of student services team that will include well-being and counselling, will probably make use of digital/online as well as in-person support, and will be well connected to local physical and mental health networks. Academic staff are briefed on how to spot students who are struggling, and personal tutors will usually be focused on the academic and personal well-being of their tutees. Student Unions also offer good support, not just on mental health but also on other aspects such as academic practice and finances. And if students are living in halls of residence, there will be wardens and other staff on hand to talk to and get help with finding the right support. There are also often buddies, mentors, and Student Ambassadors on campus and in departments to provide peer-to-peer support.

As with study Progress, it helps learners to know themselves well enough – and be honest enough with themselves – to spot when things are not going well. Lots of universities give out advice about how to spot the signs of depression or feeling isolated or overwhelmed. And it is important to recognise that the first few weeks of university present a huge multi-sensory challenge. Students are bombarded with information and experiences from all angles, and with the neuroscience in mind it is just as hard to make sense of all of that simultaneously without much to filter it through. Universities are increasingly managing the induction week experience for new students to try to make it less intense and demanding, but with all the exciting opportunities and distractions to do new things and meet new people, it is a challenge to balance out what to do and how to spend your time. Again, having a range of people to reflect on that with – including the Careers Service who will often have Student Ambassadors themselves – can help new students reflect on their priorities.

It is also always possible to take time out of a degree, suspending studies to allow for illness to pass or other situations to be resolved. It is really important for students to engage with their academic department, make the right people aware of what adjustments might be needed, and follow the procedures to make sure that their situation is properly registered. Again, there is no shame in pausing, or even in dropping out. University might have seemed like a good idea at the start, but lots of things can change. And as with all decisions, changing your mind means a longer route with more learning to draw on.

So, we can support learners to prepare to identify and take advantage of the support around them at university by helping them recognise the role played by the Attributes and Skills they have already developed in education. These might include:

Attributes

- aware of my community
- responsible for my own actions
- emotional intelligence
- self-reflective
- being aware of the bigger picture.

Skills

- Organisation and planning
- Analysis – identify risks, understand the nature of consequence, identify, break down and solve problems
- Communication – express own views, listen effectively, question effectively, build relationships.

'... that I would learn so much from other students, because they have different ways of thinking and seeing the world'

University is experienced by some students as one big peer community. Every interaction connects students with different groups of other people the same age or in similar situations. Most of them will come from other backgrounds and countries, and many of those will not be on the same course. Friendships for life are often made at university, and we draw on the diversity of perspectives throughout our lives, as well as on the networks as we make future Careers choices. Peers help figure out the curricular and the extra-curricular and at university they tend to be more integrated into the support network than in the workplace. The commonality of experience is one of the features that often attracts learners to university in the extra-curricular sense.

The networks available are often something we draw on later in life, but I encourage learners to think more analytically about what their connections reveal to them about worlds they do not necessarily want to enter. Just as it is really easy for groups of students on the same course to all apply for the same sorts of roles, likewise it is easy to ignore or dismiss a choice by a peer in your network which is completely alien to you. Concepts like Six Degrees of Separation imply that we are all ultimately closely connected, and in a globalised workplace now even more strongly connected online, and with tools like LinkedIn at our disposal, networks are tighter than ever. It might seem now to a student that they see no future value in staying in touch with that young woman on their course who is going into investment banking, but in twenty years' time she might run her own venture capital firm and our student might be setting up their own business. Respecting others' choices and learning to recognise the multiplicity of paths taken by our peers is part of truly appreciating university as an embarkation point for many future lives.

Alumni can also become part of our peer networks at university. Many academic departments and Careers Services will bring alumni back to speak to students about their work and lives after graduation, and all students are invited to join university alumni communities when they leave. In the United States, alumni communities are strong and powerful and provide very dynamic networks in employment opportunities: this is less the case in the UK, but increasingly alumni who are not able to give money to their old university will offer work experiences or mentoring. It is really beneficial to students to take advantage of these networks in both the short and longer term.

You will also want to encourage your students to return to your school or college and share their experience of university, and keep connected with their recent peers. Passing on their experiences, warts and all, is a really valuable way for your learners to explore and shape their decisions about university and whether it is right for them or not.

So, we can support learners to prepare to identify and take advantage of their peer communities at university by helping them recognise the role played by the Attributes and Skills they have already developed in education. These might include:

Attributes

- respect others
- act to benefit others
- empathy
- truthfulness
- open-mindedness.

Skills

- Communication – express ideas with nuance, express own views, listen effectively, question effectively, make accurate references, build rapport, build relationships, give constructive feedback, communicate fluently and effectively.

'... to try to balance self-discipline, having fun and taking it all in. Being present in everything is hard work but really rewarding!'

In some senses, there is no literal equivalent to professionalism in higher education, though universities usually publish codes of conduct about acceptable behaviour of various types. Students taking up places in halls or private accommodation will sign contracts about appropriate standards of behaviour, noise, cleanliness, respect for property, and so on. And universities will also have very clear guidance on all aspects of conduct, including verbal and physical abuse. Students are usually given information about this when they join, and it is available through student services and the Students Union.

The key similarity to workplace professionalism, however, is particularly in academic terms. Plagiarism and academic misconduct, such as cheating in exams, are taken incredibly seriously and can result in immediate dismissal from an institution. Having worked in universities for almost thirty years, I have seen a significant shift as students wrestle with the balance between the freedom to develop themselves intellectually and the pressure to pass exams and get good degree grades, particularly since tuition fees were implemented. The world wide web has made it absurdly easy to access the work of others, and for others to create work for students to pass of as their own: to me, this indicates both sides of this delicate balance.

A degree result that is less good than expected can be really disappointing, but in practice over the years that follow, things tend to even themselves out. That can be a really difficult thing to hear in a state of disappointment. As someone whose A Level results were a bit of a shocker, I know that was very much not a message I wanted to hear at the time. But over the passage of time, all sorts of unimagined opportunities surface and paths open up and new connections are created. Cheating because students are afraid of getting a less good result will always create more permanent damage than working as hard as they can on their own work. For many, university is not the best environment to demonstrate what they are really capable of. They may absolutely love their subject, but not be well suited to the means of demonstrating that love. But that does not mean they will not be highly successful in another context. Cheating is, therefore, quite simply not a risk worth taking.

It is also worth making a brief point about digital footprints. Social media breaks down and blurs boundaries, and students may see it very much as social and not professional. However, Six Degrees of Separation means that an employer can very easily look through their network and eventually track down a student they have met or received an application from. There are probably algorithms that can do this too. For the employer to see a job applicant in a state of disorder on their social media feed may not be the first impression that student really wants to make.

So, we can support learners to develop professionalism and appropriate behaviours at university by helping them recognise the role played by the

Attributes and Skills they have already developed in education. These might include:

Attributes

- diligence
- self-discipline
- respect for others
- appreciate consequences of my actions
- integrity.

Skills

- Creativity – create new approaches to improving performance, make appropriate use of relevant conventions
- Analysis – understand the impact of context, identify and describe how impact, attitudes, and values are created and conveyed, identify subtle differences with wider impacts, understand the nature of causation and of consequence, follow instructions, weigh options, evaluate risks
- Communication – receive feedback constructively, listen effectively, use appropriate language, understand how audience influences interpretation.

A Last Word: Uncertainty and Ambiguity

I want to wrap up this discussion of transitions and end this book by considering the importance of one key Attribute that is particularly valuable in a pandemic-shaped world: the tolerance for ambiguity and uncertainty. This has been a feature of employer needs for a few years since the last economic upheaval in 2008, and it became significantly more important in the UK recruitment market following the Brexit vote. But in an economically complex landscape made fragile and unstable by the pandemic, and against the backdrop of accelerated, creative technological innovation driven by the need to adapt to new ways of living and working, it should be of no surprise to any of us that the expectation of tolerance for all this change is now completely normalised. We all need to have this Attribute.

The World Economic Forum, which regularly reviews the top Skills needed by global employers, identified resilience, stress tolerance, and flexibility in its 2020 report on what is needed in the period to 2025.[1] While I would describe these as Attributes, they certainly underpin our ability to respond to uncertainty and ambiguity: to manage disappointment and setbacks but keep moving forward; to keep calm and focused when challenges and tensions accumulate and increase; to find different perspectives and solutions when the situation changes. In fact, there is a suite of Attributes and transferable Skills (particularly in creativity and analysis) which learners are already developing in pre-18 education that will help them manage all this uncertainty.

There is no silver bullet in this situation, and uncertainty and ambiguity are not solely features of a pandemic-shaped world. But you can develop confidence in your learners to recognise uncertainty and ambiguity in their personal situations and the wider context, and identify when they demonstrate the Attributes and the transferable Skills that help them manage it. So, here are two ideas you can share with learners that will have lifelong value, whatever the future holds.

Meet uncertainty with curiosity

- What can I discover that is new and interesting?
- How are others developing new ways to do things or new perspectives?
- When something changes, what about it is an improvement? And what might I have done differently?
- What patterns can I see in how things have changed?

- If I could invent something now that addresses a problem we face, what would it be?

Meet the unexpected with experimentation

- If my plans are threatened or stalled, what are the other ways in which I could meet my goal? What other routes could I take to the same destination?
- How many subjects are there which are related to my first choice?
- How many jobs or careers are related to my first choice?
- If I made a different choice now, what other new choices might follow that? Does that take me further away from my original choice? What do I think about that?

We do not know what the future holds. In a way that is exciting and it is also terrifying. Right now, while we cannot hope to empathise with the anxiety of this generation about their futures and what has been lost, we have all been that young person looking ahead, wondering what is out there for us. And whatever is coming, we are doing our best to prepare learners to enter it. So, I hope that you have found something in this book that will help you get more impact from all you are doing to help your learners explore and shape their futures, and ours.

Note

1 World Economic Forum. *The Future of Jobs Report 2020* (October), p. 36. Available at: http://www3.weforum.org/docs/WEF_Future_of_Jobs_2020.pdf (accessed 29 January 2021).

Appendix 1: Further reading

I hesitate to call this a bibliography, because everyone knows what they like and do not like reading. But here are some materials you might like to pick up if you want to dig down into any of this further.

Sarah-Jayne Blakemore's excellent book on the neuroscience of the teenage brain is well worth a read and full of examples that everyone can relate to. I refer to this in **Challenge 5**.

Blakemore, S.-J. (2018) *Inventing Ourselves: The Secret Life of the Teenage Brain.* London: Transworld.

It would be easy to say that a growth mindset is the only way to cope with whatever the future has to throw at us, but Carol Dweck's wide body of research gives a strong evidential case for why such a mindset is helpful, from younger learners all the way to global business leaders.

Dweck, C. (2017) *Mindset: Changing the Way You Think to Fulfil Your Potential*, 6th edition. London: Robinson, Little, Brown Book Group.

You will have your own reading lists about equality and diversity; Scott Page's book is recommended for a business recruitment take.

Page, S.E. (2019) *The Diversity Bonus: How Great Teams Pay Off in the Knowledge Economy*. Princeton, New Jersey: Princeton University Press.

The research I share in the **Skills** section of this book has already been published as a blind peer-reviewed journal article. If you want a shorter way than this book to introduce colleagues to the idea of extracting transferable Skills from academic curriculum, it's a good place to start.

Daubney, K. (2021) "Employability is not inimical to good learning": rearticulating school academic curricula to surface their employability value, *Journal of Work-Applied Management*, (special edition May 2021). You can find the article here: https://www.emerald.com/insight/content/doi/10.1108/JWAM-08-2020-0041/full/html

I refer to DeKeyser's Skill Acquisition Theory in the **Skills** section. This is really interesting and worth a read if you are curious about how Skills might be developed alongside Knowledge.

DeKeyser, R. (2015) 'Skill acquisition theory', in VanPatten, B. and Williams, J. (eds) *Theories in Second Language Acquisition: An Introduction,* 2nd edition. London: Routledge, pp. 94–112.

The Institute of Student Employers make annual surveys of recruitment and development across graduate recruiters, as well as learning from those recruiters about their apprenticeship strategies. These surveys and reports always make really useful reading for understanding the employment market.

Prospects publish reports called *What do Graduates do?* based on survey data. By definition, survey data is only a sample, but they can be illustrative of employment patterns, particularly regionally. You can find the reports on their website: https://luminate.prospects.ac.uk/what-do-graduates-do

The Future of Work Institute at Curtin University in Perth, Western Australia, does some really interesting research on how work might look, and what the impacts might be: https://www.futureofworkinstitute.com.au/

Careers Registration data collection has transformed how HE careers services function (**Careers Activity 9: Get data**). As I note in the footnote to **Careers Activity 1**, Careers Registration as a process and concept has formed the basis of diverse approaches to enabling learners to become aware of their Career readiness. I outline the background to Careers Registration in **Appendix 4**. The two key references for further reading are:

Gilworth, R. and Thambar, N. (2013) *Careers Registration: A Data Revolution* (conference presentation), AGCAS Conference, Exeter 2013 (online). Available at: www.agcas.org.uk/events/766-Biennial-Conference-2013-Exeter

For a summary of current UK university applications of the concept, visit: https://london.ac.uk/the-careers-group/careers-registration

PwC's report on the future of work to 2030 is really fascinating. Even if you find their four proposed models to be a bit extreme, what they indicate is the strongest competing factors in how work will look amid global factors. What would be fascinating is to see how PwC think those worlds might have changed since the global pandemic of 2019/20. See:

PwC (2018) *Workforce of the Future: The Competing Forces Shaping 2030.* Available at: https://www.pwc.com/gx/en/services/people-organisation/publications/workforce-of-the-future.html (accessed 29 January 2021).

The World Economic Forum publishes a lot of reports, research, and insight from global industry leaders and thinkers which are also useful for stimulating discussion. Reports, including those quoted in this book, are available here: https://www.weforum.org/reports/

In 2020, Dr Farouk Dey and Christine Cruzvergara published on LinkedIn an article proposing the future direction of university Careers service. Both have extensive experience in the US higher education system, and it may seem that the article is not specifically relevant to your work. But it is a good indicator of how much more quickly Careers education is moving now, and how much more responsive it is having to be to the landscape. See https://www.linkedin.com/pulse/five-future-directions-university-career-services-farouk-dey/ (accessed 29 January 2021).

In the Knowledge section of **Part 3: Employability**, I refer to the impact of responding to a fast-changing context in relation to learning. Some of the leading researchers on artificial intelligence and public policy co-authored a policy paper on the impact of innovation on public perceptions of AI, which I was honoured to contribute to. You can find it here: https://www.kcl.ac.uk/policy-institute/research-analysis/innovation-and-public-attitudes (accessed 29 January 2021).

The Organisation for Economic Co-operation and Development (OECD) has a Centre for Skills that does a huge amount of research and supports governments globally with Skills strategy. See http://www.oecd.org/employment/skills-and-work/. Their publications are worth exploring, including insights into how pre-18 education should prepare learners for lifelong learning:

OECD (2019) *Getting Skills Right: Future-Ready Adult Learning Systems*. Paris: OECD Publishing. Available at: https://doi.org/10.1787/9789264311756-en (accessed 29 January 2021).

It is also worth following the writing of Glenda Quintini, a senior economist at the Centre for Skills: https://oecdskillsandwork.wordpress.com/author/glendaquintini/

Appendix 2: Other words for the Three Stage Careers Journey

When I redeveloped the Three Stage Careers Journey for this book, I used Explore to capture that first stage of discovery, Encounter to capture those first interactions with employers, work, and higher education that occur in the middle phase of the journey, and Embark to signal that this is a journey. I like alliteration!

The most important thing is to choose words that are right for your learners and your environment. Here are some suggestions listed in alphabetical order:

I'm uncertain	I've got some ideas	I understand myself well
Begin	Consider	Act
Be curious	Develop	Choose
Discover	Discuss	Commit
Enquire	Encounter	Decide
Explore	Engage	Embark
Imagine	Focus	Finalise
Invent	Narrow	Follow
Investigate	Prefer	Initiate
Prepare	Question	Plan
Search	Refine	Progress
	Reflect	Pursue
	Review	

Appendix 3: Resources for virtual work experience

In **Activity 7: Make work experience meaningful**, I share some ideas about how to develop virtual work experiences for learners. Here are some more suggestions. You probably already have websites and resources you like to use for videos, podcasts, and information sheets about roles and sectors, so I will not reinvent the wheel here. But I make reference to a few ideas in Figure 15 that you might not have come across before in school or college careers work.

Situational Judgement tests (SJTs) and exercises

These are commonly used in graduate recruitment processes, both in the application stage and the final assessment centres for candidate selection. They are essentially scenarios with dilemmas attached, where applicants are given a range of possible choices. Some scenarios are based on moral or ethical situations (e.g. You see someone has left a confidential document out on a desk and gone home, what do you do?) and others focus more on motivations or aspirations (e.g. Given the option to take on a new project when you already have a successful project on the go, what would you do?).

Some learners applying for apprenticeship roles may encounter these tests in their application phases, and you can search for sector-specific test types. Learners applying for medical school will also be asked to do a SJT: you can find more information on the Medical Schools Council website, for example.

But SJTs are also incredibly useful for helping learners who have never encountered the workplace before to find out about the sorts of decisions that are made on a daily basis. They can create a fun discussion session in small groups or using online polling tools, and while usually there is clearly a 'less good' answer, the range of answers provided will stimulate a lot of discussion and thought, and can help learners understand the concept of professionalism.

I have also included Situational Judgement when looking at specific Employability assets required to do roles, because once the role or skill-specific exercises are in place, you can develop some interesting follow-up discussions around 'what if?': What if a client doesn't like what a designer has produced? What if a chef's menu proves unpopular? What if foundations for an eco-house can only be built using environmentally unfriendly concrete?

Learning about professionalism

SJTs are also an introduction to what it means to be professional, to act appropriately in the workplace. That applies to any job or Career outcome, at whatever level in any sector, whether employed or self-employed. As with SJTs, introducing and talking about professionalism can stimulate some lively discussion, and there are some useful reference point articles on websites like Glassdoor, LinkedIn, as well as on some more specific US sites like Study.com.

It can also be really insightful to ask any employers or professionals you are working with to record a quick video on their phone to highlight three or four characteristics or behaviours that they focus on and like to see in colleagues, employees, or even clients. You can ask for general behaviours like punctuality or respect, or using appropriate language in communications, as well as more role- or sector-specific behaviours like 'cleaning up after my work is done' or 'keeping my work area tidy'. You can include these questions in panel events and Q&A sessions as well as questionnaires.

Day-in-the-life videos

If you are finding the right sort of video content hard to come by, and if you have a group of employers, local businesses, alumni, and parents who are willing, you could ask them to make some short videos for you which chronicle a day in their working life. They might show a combination of communications activities (meetings, email, phone calls, visits, surveys), organisation (organisation of events, purchasing, administration), creative activity, problem-solving, and decision-making. If possible, they should also show the workplace where possible, equipment, and any specialist Skills in action, as well as giving a feel for the rhythm of the day. It is not a small undertaking but only need be done once by each employer and you can then build up a library of resources you can use for discussion. As with all the other employer activities in this book, pre-briefing employers on what you want them to get across is really important, so that you get a learning resource that learners will benefit from within the way your programme is structured.

Learners interview employers

Online learning can be a very agile tool, but sometimes the best approach is the most direct one. Panel events and Q&As via Teams, Zoom, or Skype offer a structured way for you to shape employer/learner interactions, but learners in the Encounter and Embark stages will need the chance to dig down into the detail. Again, getting permission to record these in some way, or create transcripts at least, is a really valuable way to get a permanent resource. If there is any possibility of the employer talking a small group of learners through a typical work task, asking key questions of the learners as they explore the task, then that provides the nearest virtual version of an in-person work experience that you could get. Again, preparation on both sides is important: learners should go into an interview like this having read up, watched videos, and thought about what they need to learn that will help them make progress with their Careers journeys. If possible, they can identify a typical work task they would like to go through with an employer so that they can really benefit.

Interviews also place onus on the learner to take responsibility for the learning gain they want to make, which is a good habit to establish. On the employer side, helping them understand the role of this interview for learners' Careers journeys will help keep it focused: we all know how big and complicated jobs are, so sharing questions in advance can help the employer stay on topic and really add value to a live conversation (even if you then record it!).

Problem-based learning

Many universities globally now use problem-based learning as a core element in how curriculum is delivered, including across professionally aligned courses like medicine as well as cross-disciplinary groups across different subjects. In a way, it is a bit misleading to describe it as being focused on a 'problem' because that implies there is a solution. In practice, this approach is often about mapping multiple solutions, exploring options, and weighing up pros and cons. This is particularly effective when it is done in small groups rather than with individual learners, because it enables a range of perspectives. Fundamental workplace Skills like identifying core factors in a situation, prioritising needs or actions, and mapping out steps in a process surface quickly through these sorts of activities.

A key challenge can be finding authentic problems, so this is where employers you are working with can really help. If they are big enough to have their own professional development team or online learning library for staff, then they may well have introductory level material they can share. If they are small or self-employed, then their own training materials from when they qualified are likely to offer useful ideas. Employers can also create their own scenarios:

- Water is spraying out of the floor in an upstairs bedroom – How do I figure out where the problem is?
- A cosmetic company wants to sell more shampoo but also wants to cut back on its plastic footprint – What are the options?

These problems are not just useful for learners interested in a particular Career. They help learners understand how many transferable Skills are required for dissecting problems, asking good questions, and exploring solutions.

Another source of problem-based learning comes from the Management Consultancy sector. Assessment processes for graduates entering the sector often involve case studies and while some are quite specific, the more general types can introduce learners to thinking not only about the problem itself, but why problems like that need to be solved in the workplace.

Brainteasers

- For example, how many golf balls fit inside a jumbo jet?
  - This is an estimation task, but after talking through the problem, and figuring out what pieces of information would be required to

solve the problem, you can also discuss what scenarios estimation is useful in, e.g. how many beds you might fit in a hospital ward, or how many potatoes to buy for a roast dinner for forty people.

Market Sizing

- For example, what is the market for specialist doughnut shops in the UK?
  - o This is a different kind of estimation task, because it involves looking not just at numbers but also qualitative evidence like behaviours, preferences, and choice. Discussion can follow about different roles where people have to combine quantitative choice (how many of these items can we stock?) with qualitative choice (how popular will these items be, and why?). That is also really useful for any learners thinking about setting up their own business or being a freelancer.

Again, if you have employers or professionals you work with already, you can ask them to provide examples of cases like these where they have had to work out the scale of a problem to solve and how to go about solving it.

Role-specific and Skill-specific tasks and simulations

If an employer has a typical work task they can share with you, either for running by you or through interaction with them via a virtual meetings platform, then that's great, and you can begin to build up a library of tasks of your own. For example:

- A designer interviews a client to identify their design project needs:
  - o The learners do not need to be studying design because this focuses on client relationship management, developing communication Skills including effective questioning and listening
- A restaurant manager has to decide on a new menu with a chef: what are the considerations for choosing a new menu?
  - o The learners are focusing on identifying and weighing up options and choice, and – as with the market sizing case study – exploring how that impacts decision-making and priorities
- A nurse has a number of tasks on the ward: which order should they be done in?
  - o Learning about prioritisation and the impact of decisions on other people is key to being effective in the workplace
- Building a sustainable and eco-friendly house: how should materials be chosen?
  - o Reconciling ambition with reality is a key element of work: parameters such as cost are weighed against how sustainable the materials should be and their longevity.

Roleplay

Interviews and videos give you a great resource from which to develop learner roleplays for different roles and careers. If you have a particularly enthusiastic employer, you might ask them to let the learner play their part and they play the client or colleague. But this also works well where learners reflect on what they have learned and then develop conversations focused on specific Skills or roleplays in pairs or small groups. For example:

- A dentist has to persuade a scared patient to have an injection before a filling
- A politician has to see the point of view of their constituent
- A logistics manager has to decide which food items should be delivered in which order
- A clothes designer has to create a jumpsuit for a man that is multifunctional for different climates: how can the design be adapted?

As with all these exercises, reflection is essential:

- How has this experience helped me understand what doing this job is really like?
- What would it be like doing that every day?
- Where are the challenges for me and what is easier for me?

Appendix 4: Career readiness: The backstory

In the early 2010s, Dr Bob Gilworth and Dr Nalayini Thambar of the Careers Centre at the University of Leeds developed a way to identify where students at Leeds were on their Career journey.[1] This simple set of questions was embedded into annual study registration processes at the university and created a dataset which enabled Bob, Nalayini, and the Leeds Careers team to identify which students on which programmes and in which years of study were at which stages of their Career planning, and to target resource and interventions more effectively. This process, called Career Registration, also established an annual dataset that generated patterns of readiness: how did the Career readiness of individual students and cohorts of students change year by year, and where were interventions most effective?

This concept has revolutionised the way that higher education Careers services track the needs of their students, and around two-thirds of UK universities now use Careers Registration processes, as well as an increasing number in Australia and New Zealand.

Of the many universities that now use Careers Registration, some have simplified the number of questions, and several now identify three main phases in a Careers journey, which might be roughly described as:

- I don't have much of an idea of what I want to do
- I have some ideas but no plan for proceeding any of them
- I know what I want to do and I have a plan to do it.

The only disadvantage of the original process behind Careers Registration is that it only happens annually, so students can easily forget how they answered the question originally, and they may also change their mind several times during the year. But the phases of Career readiness remain the same all year round. So, when the University of London appointed me to be Head of Careers & Employability at King's, I took two steps to try to maximise the benefit of Bob and Nalayini's original concept of Careers Registration.

Firstly, as occurred in a number of other university Careers services using Careers Registration, for the version of the process we used at King's College

London, I labelled the stages or phases. But I then took that clarification a step further, creating explanations of how a student at a particular stage might experience an activity. This is equivalent to the pedagogical approach of creating context-dependent learning outcomes. For example, if you are in the first phase, you will benefit from a Careers guidance appointment because it will help you explore your options. Whereas if you are in the final stage, you will use that same appointment very differently, to refine how you take your plans forward. That means that every time a student sees the words that label their Careers stage, they can immediately self-identify which stage of their Careers journey they are at. And when they are considering which of the Careers activities or services to use, they can see how it will help them in different ways, depending on where they are on their Career journey.

The other development was to ask students after those interactions to tell us where they had been on their Careers journey before the interaction, and where they were after it. Again, this is standard reflective practice, applied to Careers education. It creates a mini-Careers Registration survey and, being interaction-based not annual, it gives the student an immediate reflection opportunity that reinforces the concept of readiness and the learning gain of the interaction. So, when numerical values are attached to the before and after answers, it also generates data that helps the team see where the interventions are impactful. In one sample year, 85 per cent of students made progress in their understanding of Employability after a guidance appointment. That is evidence which is very hard to argue with.

You can find out more about the Careers Registration process through the guide created by The Careers Group of The University of London, who hosted a nationally funded project to interpret data about student Career readiness: https://london.ac.uk/the-careers-group/careers-registration

Note

1   The official reference source for this is given in Appendix 1. However, at the time of writing, this is a difficult resource to access for non-members of AGCAS, so to get insight into how this approach is now being used, visit https://london.ac.uk/the-careers-group/careers-registration

Appendix 5: Employability and KASE: The backstory

There are two ways to tell this story. From the perspective of educators and from the perspective of learners.

This narrative describes some work I was appointed to create while deployed by the University of London to be Head of King's Careers & Employability at King's College London. A research-led university, like King's, with generally high proportions of good quality graduate employment doesn't seem like the obvious place to embed Employability in the curriculum. Research-led teaching and curriculum are not obviously aligned with courses that are strongly Career-led, although at King's around half of students are training for health professions, including medicine, dentistry, and nursing. But research-led teaching and curriculum also tend to be highly focused on the in-depth study of those subjects, and adding Employability-focused content doesn't always seem logical or coherent with the academic curriculum, particularly in subjects which are not professionally aligned. Furthermore, it can feel like a lot of extra work for academic colleagues to bring additional content into the curriculum, as it often requires making other content optional, finding additional time for teaching, or leaving other content out. That said, everyone can agree that we want students to enjoy their degree and benefit from it in the longer term. So, finding a way to develop students' Employability without sacrificing or compromising the degree experience in other ways is a complex problem.

From the student's point of view, as we have considered in **Challenge 5**, university is often a high-risk and uncertain phase, combining the last opportunity to study for study's sake with the knowledge that higher education has to provide some sort of effective gateway into future work. And that high-risk phase has considerable financial and time commitment attached. As a transition, it ought to be a powerful and effective one, but the open-mindedness of employers to the degree subjects their future employees have studied can seem confusing to students: 'If employers aren't that choosy about what I've studied, how do I communicate the value of a choice which was really important to me but I'm not sure of its value to employers? What are they looking for? And even if I know what they are looking for in terms of Skills and competences, how do I know that I've got them in sufficient quantities if I haven't been able to get the right work experience for one reason or another?'

And what about those students for whom getting to university *was* the destination but who aren't yet ready to think beyond that? What about those students who perhaps, despite your best efforts as Careers professionals, haven't engaged much with Careers activities at school and do not feel confident to engage with the university Careers Service either. 'You only go to the Careers Service if you know what you want to do, right?' How can we as educators be sure they are ever going to develop their Employability if they can choose not to do so?

With those two points of view in mind, I had to find a way to make it unavoidable for students to develop their Employability, no matter what the course was, who the student was, or how interested the academic colleague was in Employability. I couldn't change the curriculum, and I couldn't add to it or take away from it. But at least I could be sure that if we did something with or through the curriculum, every student would engage with it, because it is the only thing every student engages with. Besides, we know that employers want graduates. Something is happening during that educational experience that turns students into future employees. So, let's see what that is.

Extracted Employability was born from me reading in detail every curriculum document that forms the backbone of higher education in the UK, as published by the Quality Assurance Agency. The Subject Benchmark Statements are written by academics for academics to outline what the Knowledge content of UK degrees should be. But each of them, in their different ways, also comments on the Attributes and transferable Skills and Experiences that surface in different ways through the teaching. The introduction to the Statements also says that they are intended to support you if you are 'an employer, to find out about the knowledge and skills generally expected of a graduate in this subject'. I'm not aware of any employer who has read these Statements, but the intention is clear: in higher education curriculum, employers will find what they are looking for (and therefore 'who').

So, I developed a way to make that much clearer to students, academics, and employers. Extracting Employability from the curriculum literally takes the curriculum as it is taught – the content, the scope, the learning outcomes, the programme design – and surfaces its innate Employability value in terms of Knowledge, Attributes, Skills, and Experience (KASE), the precise elements that employers are looking for. Sometimes Knowledge overlaps with specific Career paths and sometimes it doesn't. I identified over 200 transferable Skills and 80 Attributes in the Statements, with which I gave academics and students a rich and powerful language to say with much greater clarity how an innately academic education also prepares students for the workplace in exactly the way that employers want.

You can find out more about the detail of my higher education research in a forthcoming peer-reviewed academic journal article published in *Higher Education, Skills, and Work-Based Learning*.

In 2019, I began a new independent piece of research to evaluate pre-18 curriculum in the UK. I asked, does any Employability value exist in that curriculum documentation? What are the transferable Skills innate to each academic subject? While not all pre-18 learners go into work, a huge proportion do, and we know that employers are often not seeking learners with particular subject combinations. The findings of my research evolved into SkillsMap® and I believe they give us a completely new way to talk about the Employability value of pre-18 traditional academic curriculum, not just in the UK but anywhere in the world. As I describe in the Skills section of **Part 3: Employability**, this research demonstrates that each subject has a suite of transferable Skills embedded into it, which simply need surfacing to learners. You can read more about the research in my peer-reviewed journal article, and by visiting yourskillsmap.com:

Daubney, K. (2021) 'Employability is not inimical to good learning': Rearticulating school academic curricula to surface their employability value, *Journal of Work-Applied Management* (forthcoming in special edition May 2021). Available at: https://www.emerald.com/insight/content/doi/10.1108/JWAM-08-2020-0041/full/html

Index

Note to the reader: This is a book about Careers, Employability, learner and learnings, Skills, curriculum, work experience and many other themes, so some of the index listings are quite long. In the case of Learners and Skills I would be listing most of the pages in the book because they are core elements to the book, so they do not have generic entry listings. That said, I have tried to make this index as usable as possible, to help you navigate the complex interconnection of the themes.